W9-AHX-097

CROSS STITCH
COUNTRY
GARDEN

CROSS STITCH
COUNTRY
GARDEN
—— JANE ILES ——

David & Charles

DEDICATION

To the memory of my uncle, William Dow

A DAVID & CHARLES BOOK

First published in the UK in 1996

Text, designs and charts Copyright © Jane Iles 1996
Photography and layout Copyright © David & Charles 1996

Jane Iles has asserted her right to be identified as author
of this work in accordance with the Copyright,
Designs and Patents Act, 1988.

A catalogue record for this book is available from the
British Library.

ISBN 0 7153 0332 5

Photography by Di Lewis
Book design by Margaret Foster

Printed in Spain by Graficus Reunidas. SA
for David & Charles
Brunel House   Newton Abbot   Devon

Contents

Introduction

LOWERS AND GARDENS NEVER fail to inspire me and country gardens in particular intrigue me with their abundance of wonderful plant life – the way they pass serenely through the seasons and how, year after year, they play an important role in our everyday lives.

What could be more satisfying than to see cheerful lines of laundry drying in the clean country air, billowing like the sails of an old ship. How comforting it is to see orderly rows of vegetables standing to attention in the vegetable patch, their roots, fruits and leaves swelling ready for the kitchen table. The sight of vigorous clumps of brash herbaceous flowers has always evoked exciting ideas, as do the brightly jewelled surprises of aconites and hellebores that bring hope during the harsh winter months.

With such wonderfully thought-provoking images in my mind I decided to use cross stitch as the method by which to translate these images into fabric and thread, to explore a country garden through the seasons and discover its many traits.

Just as I find gardens so inspiring, I also find the process of cross-stitch design stimulating. It is an uncluttered and extremely rewarding medium, as it passes from the initial stages of selecting the subject, through sketching and drawing to simplifying and charting the design onto graph paper. I still prefer to design on paper with pencil and crayon, rather than on computer, although there are instances when the computer can speedily give assistance.

I am sure my journey through a country garden, revealing as it does such a wealth of flowers, fruits and vegetables, will inspire you to create many of the projects in this book. The simple construction of cross stitch will allow even the novice to produce satisfyingly beautiful objects, while for the more accomplished embroiderer there is scope to experiment and extend many of my designs and create a whole country garden of your own.

Before You Begin...

One of the joys of cross-stitch embroidery is that you do not need vast amounts of materials or equipment to succeed. Another big plus is that cross stitch is technically simple, requiring only basic skills and techniques. This section is important as it describes the materials and equipment needed and then tells you how to master the skills required to complete the gorgeous projects that follow.

MATERIALS & EQUIPMENT

*MATERIALS AND EQUIPMENT are minimal for cross stitch. For the novice it is
probably a good idea to initially choose a small design to stitch, then only
small quantities of fabric and threads are required, plus perhaps a small frame or
hoop, although this is not vital as small-scale cross stitch can be hand held.
Some of the projects in this book require specific items to display the embroidery,
such as trinket boxes, pincushions, card mounts and footstools. Suppliers
for these are suggested on page 127.*

FABRICS

Cross stitch is a form of counted thread embroidery which can be worked on a great variety of fabrics, although it is usual and generally more effective to use an evenweave fabric with threads that are easy to count. For freestyle and experimental cross stitch other less traditional fabrics can be used but for the projects within this book I have chosen only evenweaves that are popular and easily obtainable.

As the name evenweave suggests the fabric is evenly constructed with the weft threads passing regularly over the warp threads so that when cross stitches are worked the stitches are well-balanced in shape and size, similar to the squares of the grid or chart from which the designs are taken.

Evenweave fabrics are often described as having a particular 'count' or gauge. This is the method used to differentiate between the various fabrics. Those with a high count are fine and can be used for very detailed cross stitching; those with a lower count are for bolder, less complicated stitchery.

The choice of evenweave fabric is vast, although some are very expensive and others not always easily available. They are predominantly made from either cotton or linen fibres.

The cotton fabrics are generally known as Aidas. There are a growing number of colours, effects and counts for you to choose from making this range very desirable as there is a fabric to suit all abilities and most designs. From the novice or child to the expert stitcher, all can be satisfied. It is a shame that some people may have dismissed Aida as being a fabric reminiscent of school needlework lessons; they should think again and try some of the more unusual types offered today.

The linen fabrics are much more expensive than the cottons, but the beautiful and very satisfying results that can be achieved justify the extra investment. However, I would suggest that the beginner should avoid using linen fabric at first as the grid pattern that is so clearly woven into the Aida fabric is not present in the plain weave of the linen. For those who wish to use a less expensive linen-type fabric there are now several available made from cotton or cotton mixes (see Linda below).

The following fabrics have been used in this book; they are also the ones I enjoy using most. Remember you can always substitute a specific fabric with another of similar gauge. You can also, with some experimentation, deliberately alter the size of your cross-stitch embroidery by choosing a coarser or finer fabric to make it bigger or smaller.

Aida (Zweigart E3706) 14-count: This cotton fabric is woven with threads grouped in even blocks or sets with clearly spaced holes between the sets of threads. 14-count Aida is enjoyable to use as it allows designs to be quite detailed, while at the same time it is easy on the eye and quite quick to work.

Gold/Fleck Aida (Zweigart E3287) 14-count: This is similar to the fabric above but has the luxury of a Lurex thread woven into it. It is particularly effective when used for items such as Christmas decorations and cards. It has the added attraction of being available in small ready-cut pieces.

Aida (Zweigart E1007) 11-count: With fewer sets of threads per inch (2.5cm) this Aida gives larger, bolder stitches.

Hardanger (Zweigart E1008) 22-count: The sets or blocks of threads in this cotton fabric are grouped in pairs. It produces very fine cross stitches and you can also work your stitches over two horizontal and two vertical pairs of threads to give only eleven bolder stitches per inch (2.5cm).

Linda (Zweigart E1235) 27-count: This is a finely woven cotton fabric where the weft and warp threads are individually woven single threads, unlike those above which are in sets or blocks. It is similar to linen and when cross stitches are worked over two horizontal and two vertical threads, giving fourteen stitches per inch (2.5cm), the effect is very pleasing.

Single thread or mono canvas (Zweigart E1281) 14-count: This is a white single-weave canvas. It is used for the footstool on page 74 and the cross stitches are worked over two horizontal and two vertical threads so that there are only seven stitches per inch (2.5cm), producing a quick-growing yet rich effect.

Scalloped-edge Aida band (Zweigart E7107, E7195): There is an increasing selection of Aida (and linen) bands available, in different widths and colours, many with decorative edgings. The Aida bands give an even number of stitches across their width while the linen bands give an odd number.

Perforated or stitching paper 14-count: Punched paper with regular rows of holes was very popular with the Victorians and is regaining popularity, offering a very different ground upon which to stitch. It can be most effective when used to produce small items such as bookmarks, needle cases, small book covers, greetings cards and small boxes. Once stitched it can be cut to shape and glued, sculpted or folded. Care must be taken when handling the paper as it will spoil if accidentally folded, crumpled or soiled and will tear if worked roughly. Remember you are using a very different medium to that of your evenweave fabric. Paper does not have the same soft and pliable quality and will be damaged permanently if handled without respect. Before you begin your design, carefully plan how much perforated paper you really need to use as the excess will have to be trimmed off and probably discarded.

Folding paper is not advisable unless it is part of your design as any creasing is permanent so once more plan how you are going to work and handle the paper. Roll the paper if this will help you to hold it efficiently.

THREADS

There are, of course, a great many threads available today but DMC stranded cotton (floss) has been used throughout this book, with the exception of the footstool on page 74 which uses DMC tapestry wools. You can select your threads from the Anchor or Madeira ranges but I suggest you choose them carefully in natural daylight, selecting colours that work well together for a particular project. Do remember, it is not always possible to achieve a perfect colour match from one brand to another: there are some colours which simply cannot be substituted because of their unique shades. While conversion charts are readily available to help you make substitutions it is always advisable to look in daylight at your selected threads and ask yourself if the colours are effective when put together. Do not be afraid to ask the shop assistant to allow you to look at the threads in natural light; some shops have extremely poor lighting in which we are expected to make our choice of fabrics and yarns.

DMC stranded cotton (floss): Made up of six strands of mercerised cotton, this can be used as a single strand or in any combination to give different thicknesses. Three strands are used to work the cross stitches throughout this book, though for finer detail, such as the wings of the bumble bees in the Summer Roses Cushion on page 42, only two strands are used.

DMC tapestry (tapisserie) wool: This is a non-divisible four-ply woollen yarn, ideal for canvaswork and available in a range of beautiful colours.

DMC coton perlé No 5 thread: This non-divisible twisted thread has a rich, shiny appearance. I have used it to make twisted cords to embellish some of the projects.

DMC divisible metallic thread: A bright and sparkly three-strand thread on a spool, this is available in a range of metallic colours.

EQUIPMENT

Most of the equipment needed for making the projects will probably already be in your sewing basket – a good pair of sharp, pointed trimming scissors, larger dressmaking shears, paper-cutting scissors, a good selection of various sized needles (some with round points or blunt-ended for your embroidery), thimbles, dressmaking pins, a tape measure, ruler and tacking (basting) threads. In addition to these there are also a few special items that will greatly assist you.

NEEDLES

As with any other form of counted thread embroidery you will need blunt-ended (also described as tapestry) needles for your cross stitching. The blunt end of the needle allows you to pass the embroidery yarn smoothly through the holes in the fabric without splitting the woven threads. If you have a variety of different sizes at hand you can select which is best for each piece of embroidery. I like to use a Size 26 needle for most of my three-strand cross stitching and occasionally a Size 24 needle with thicker yarns, and larger still for use with wool on canvas (see footstool, page 74).

Never leave your needle in the working part of the fabric: secure it safely at one edge or in a needle case as over time any moisture may cause the needle to rust and cause permanent staining to your embroidery fabric.

HOOPS AND FRAMES

Whether or not you use a hoop or frame is a matter of personal choice. I much prefer to use something to hold my fabric flat and taut as it is kept looking fresh, crumple-free and not in need of laundering afterwards. The main disadvantage is that you have to allow plenty of fabric around the area to be stitched for mounting.

I have suggested the type and size of frame or hoop used in each project, but you can of course choose something different. Certainly when working the larger projects you will find a frame beneficial.

Embroidery hoops: These can be used for small cross-stitch designs which fit comfortably within the size of the hoop. Wooden hoops are preferable to the less rigid plastic ones and many different sizes are available. They are inexpensive so you can build up a collection of different sizes. Winding fabric tape around the outer hoop not only keeps the stretched fabric taut within the hoop but also protects it from the hard wooden edge. Always make sure the grain of the fabric is straight within the hoop.

Rectangular frames: These are made from lengths of whitewood, ¾ x ¾in (2 x 2cm), with mitred or butted corners, held together with wood glue and nails. I have made a selection of these, finding them useful, durable and inexpensive. Old softwood picture frames or artists' stretchers can also be used. Embroidery frames similar in principle to artists' stretchers are becoming popular as they are sold in pairs of sides so you can select the exact size you require. The sides are temporarily slotted together to make the frame. Then when the embroidery is removed, the frame can be dismantled and reused to make a frame of different size and proportion.

The fabric is stretched and fastened to the frame with staples or drawing pins (thumb tacks). Start at the centre of opposite sides and work towards the corners, carefully pulling and fixing the fabric so that it is secure on the frame, evenly taut and most importantly, the grain is straight.

Rotating frames: These are more expensive but can be useful as they are adjustable. They are available in different sizes but for the projects in this book a small 12in (30cm) frame is used. This allows you to embroider long, thin strips for the borders of towels, bed linen and table place settings, keeping the excess fabric neatly rolled up on the rotating sides of the frame, leaving the area to be worked flat and quite taut.

G-CRAMP

When using a rectangular frame I work much more quickly if I have both hands free to stitch with. If you attach the frame to the edge of a table with a carpenter's G-cramp or C-clamp you will free both hands and improve your posture, reducing the risk of backache. Remember to protect the table from the cramp with a small piece of thick fabric or cardboard to avoid damaging a wooden surface.

SEWING MACHINE

If you own or have access to a sewing machine you will find it very helpful when making up many of the items, as it is both time and labour saving. A modern machine, which has both straight and satin (zigzag) stitch facilities, is ideal. Decorative edging stitches are useful though not essential. If you are unsure of a technique using the sewing machine always practise on spare fabric to gain confidence.

CARE OF EMBROIDERY

If you have used good quality fabrics and threads, your embroidery will last for years. However, here are some tips to ensure its life is prolonged.

❦ While you are embroidering a design always make sure your hands are clean and fresh, especially in hot sticky weather, to safeguard against soiling your fabric and threads.

❦ Do not leave embroidery in progress, exposed to bright sunshine and other potential hazards. Cats (and children) seem to have a magnetic attraction towards partially worked embroidery with possibly disastrous results. Temporarily cover your work with a clean cloth (tea towel) and always store it in a suitable bag.

❦ Take care not to expose embroidery to bright light (natural or artificial) and do not place it close to a heat source or in a damp atmosphere. These conditions can fade the colours and weaken the fibres.

❦ If articles require laundering (such as special-occasion towels, bed and table linen), use a mild cleaning agent and gentle washing action. Reshape the article carefully while damp and press on the wrong side before it is completely dry.

❦ Dry cleaning (by a specialist) is highly recommended for any item that you fear may not be totally colourfast or shrink-proof.

❦ Always treat your embroidery with loving care and respect. A gentle brush or shake will keep the dust at bay (the upholstery attachment of the vacuum cleaner may be used with care).

❦ If you have to store embroidery for a long time store it flat or rolled (folding will crease fabric permanently and in time may break the fibres). Always wrap in layers of acid-free tissue paper, then place it in a clean fabric, Cellophane or paper bag (not plastic). Put it somewhere dark, dry and of course moth-free. I store much of my embroidery in strong cardboard boxes with a liberal scattering of herbal moth-repellent sachets which have a light and pleasant aroma.

BASIC STITCHES & TECHNIQUES

Cross-stitch embroidery is technically simple – anyone can do it with a little practice. Soon you will gain skills and confidence and find your own way of doing things. I hope the following points will help you to enjoy working the embroidery and making up the projects in this book.

THE STITCHES

CROSS STITCH

Cross stitch is worked in two stages, with two diagonal stitches being worked over each other to form a cross. It is important to work all the crosses so that the upper stitches face the same way to create a smooth and even effect. The tension of the thread is important – too loose and the crosses will appear untidy, too tight and they will pinch the fabric, unevenly distorting both fabric and stitch. I find the use of a frame always encourages even cross stitches. Work neatly and try to keep the wrong side free from knots, tails and loops.

Whether you work from left to right or right to left is unimportant. Also, whether you fill an area by working each stitch completely or partially, going back over it once you have filled the area in half stitches, is really up to individual preference.

For the novice, it is probably a good idea to work a trial sample on a spare piece of evenweave fabric to become familiar with the stitch. Work several rows in different directions. Also try some small, uneven shapes, practising how you can travel through the shape in the best path. Soon you will feel confident with your tension and method of working.

TO WORK A CROSS STITCH

1 The easiest method of starting off is to position the knot on the right side a short distance away from where your first stitch will be. When the thread under the fabric has been covered by stitches the knot can be carefully and tidily snipped off.

2 Look at your fabric as if it is a grid (Aida is the best fabric for this), then select where you want a cross to be (think of it as filling a square on a grid). Bring the needle up at the bottom right corner of your square and take it down at the top left corner so that the thread lies diagonally across the square or group of threads.

3 Next, bring the needle up at the bottom left corner and then down at the top right, making the second diagonal to complete the cross stitch (see Fig 1a).

Sometimes it is a good idea to half work some of your cross stitches. For example if you are building up an irregular shape which has long thin arms to it then you

will use your thread more economically and neatly by working only the first half of each cross stitch outwards and then completing the crosses with the second half as you return back over the first stitches (see Fig 1b).

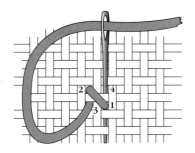

Fig 1a Working a single cross stitch

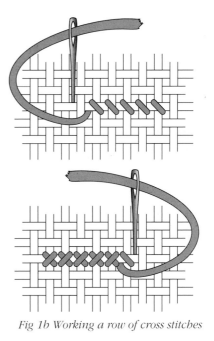

Fig 1b Working a row of cross stitches

BACK STITCH

This can be used to outline a shape, for example the delicate wings of the bumble bees on the Summer Roses Cushion on page 42 and the Rose-scented Sachet on page 45. You can vary the strength of definition by the thickness of thread. Worked horizontally, vertically or diagonally, back stitches are usually the same size as the cross stitches. However, you can achieve more detail if you use fewer strands of thread to make the stitches smaller and ignore the grid-like pattern of the fabric.

TO WORK BACK STITCH

1 Bring the thread up on the line to be sewn, making the first stitch backwards, from left to right.

2 Pass the needle down through the fabric, a little in front of the first stitch and make another stitch, inserting the needle at the point where it first came through. Repeat and continue in this way along the line in a right or left direction as shown in Fig 2.

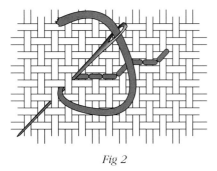

Fig 2

FRENCH KNOTS

These work well with cross-stitch embroidery as they give an added dimension to the level and even stitchery (see the Summer Roses Cushion, page 42). The knots are added last and randomly to give a raised texture.

TO WORK A FRENCH KNOT

1 Bring the needle up to the right side of the fabric at the required position, hold the thread down with the left thumb and wind the thread around the needle twice (see Fig 3a). Still holding the thread, pass the needle back down through the fabric, one thread or part of a block

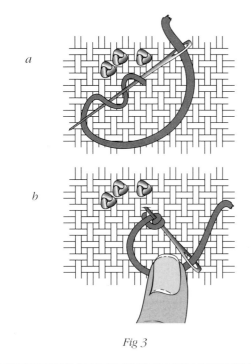

a

b

Fig 3

away from where it came (see Fig 3b). (If you pass the needle down where it first came up the knot will be pulled through to the wrong side.)

2 Pull the thread through to the back and secure for a single French knot or pass across the back of the fabric for a further stitch.

THE TECHNIQUES

MAKING A TWISTED CORD

I like to finish off many of my designs by adding a twisted cord that picks out one of the colours used in the embroidery.

The cords are easy to make and you can select whatever colour you like. Sometimes it is quite difficult and expensive to purchase a suitable matching cord.

1 Cut the required number of lengths of coton perlé thread. (As a rough guide the length must be 2½ to 3 times longer than the finished length required – allow more rather than less.)

2 Knot the lengths together at one end and loop this around a closed door or window handle (or get a friend to hold it very firmly).

3 Knot the other ends together and pass a pencil through the loop. Keeping the thread taut, wind the pencil round and round so that the thread twists, eventually coiling around itself. Now it can be slackened slightly.

4 Carefully bring the two knotted ends together so that both halves of the thread twist around one another. Gently pull and ease the cord until it is evenly twisted.

5 Knot the ends together to prevent them from unravelling. Trim the ends beyond the knots leaving approximately ⅜in (1cm) and with a pin or needle gently unravel the threads teasing out the fibres to look like mock tassels.

MAKING A TWO-COLOUR TWISTED CORD

1 Use two groups of different coloured thread of the required length. Tie all the threads together at one end, to join the two colours.

2 Now separate the colours so that the knot lies at the centre with one colour on one side of it and the second colour on the other. This doubles the length of the threads to be twisted.

3 Knot the loose ends of each colour and make the cord in the way described above.

MAKING A FOLD-OVER CARD

To make your own gift or greetings card first choose thin card that is firm enough to stand up when the embroidery is mounted within it. There is an increasing selection of unusually textured paper and card (some hand-made) now available in good art and craft shops which are wonderful for making fold-over cards, adding to the unique quality of your embroidered greetings card.

1 Calculate the size you require for the front of the card – this means the size of the window or aperture needed *plus* a border. If unsure make a trial card with spare paper. Draw this shape on your chosen card three times in a row. The result will look like a three-part panel (see Fig 4).

2 Score the fold lines lightly (see fold lines on Fig 4) but do not fold yet.

3 Draw the aperture shape in the correct position on the central panel then cut out using a sharp craft knife and non-slip steel ruler on a cutting mat.

4 Position the aperture over your embroidery, trimming away any excess fabric. Use fabric glue or double-sided adhesive tape to stick the embroidery into position.

5 The right-hand side of the card (A) is now folded behind the mounted embroidery and glued in position and the left-hand side (B) is folded to become the back of the card on which you can write your message.

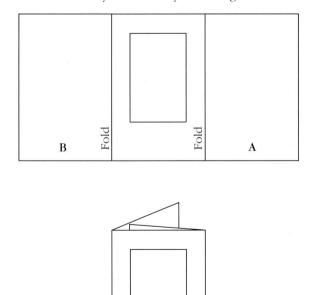

Fig 4

STRETCHING AND MOUNTING FABRIC ON CARDBOARD

Always use rigid cardboard, otherwise it will bend when the fabric is pulled tightly around it. If possible use white acid-free board, or add a layer of acid-free tissue paper to reduce the risk of damage to you fabric.

1 Carefully measure the size your mount needs to be and cut the cardboard on an old board or cutting mat, using a very sharp craft knife and a non-slip steel ruler. Check that the mount will fit within the frame.

2 On a clean, flat surface place your embroidered fabric right-side down, then put the cardboard on top, centring it. If there is a lot of excess fabric trim some away but remember you need to leave approximately 1¼in (3cm) to be turned to the back of the cardboard.

3 Carefully lift up the cardboard and the fabric, then replace it on the flat surface making sure the embroidery is still in the correct position with the cardboard behind it. With large-headed dressmaker's pins (glass-headed are ideal) and working along opposite sides simultaneously, gently pull the fabric to stretch it. Hold it by inserting the pins into the narrow edge of the cardboard. Do not push the pins in far, just enough to hold the fabric in place. Check the embroidery is positioned correctly before pinning the remaining two sides.

4 Use a long, double length of buttonhole thread to lace the opposite edges of the fabric together on the back of the cardboard. Work from the centres towards the corners, pulling the threads tightly and evenly. Make sure you secure the threads well and only do so if you are satisfied with your work. Remove all the pins along the laced sides and repeat with the other two sides. The fabric at the corners can be tucked in neatly and laced in position.
NOTE: Do not pull the buttonhole thread vigorously or too tightly as it can rip the fabric.

MAKING UP ITEMS BY HAND

I have recommended the use of a sewing machine in several of the projects as it will save a great deal of time and labour and produce a neater, more professional result. However, some of the small projects such as the herb pillows, can be made up by hand. You can substitute machine straight stitch with either running or back stitch. Machine satin (zigzag) stitch can be substituted by hand satin stitch and buttonhole stitch can be worked along a cut edge to prevent it fraying. Remember you will probably be working through several layers of fabric so make sure that the needle passes through all of them, neatly and efficiently. In some cases you may find this quite difficult, however with patience and perseverance it can be achieved.

CHAPTER 1

The Garden in Springtime

THE RICH, JEWEL-LIKE colours of the spring-flowering anemone will cheer any heart after the dull days of winter and it was the vivid scarlets, mauves, inky-blues and purples that inspired me to draw these delightful flowers. A single flower grew to many and then on to a garland and then a whole border. The result is this simple but stunningly effective anemone motif which has been used as the basis of The Garden in Springtime collection. The projects derived from it include colourful towel borders, scented sachets and an anemone cushion.

The basic design is eye-catching with bold splashes of petal colour contrasting with feathery foliage to give a satisfying visual balance. Strong but flexible repetition works equally well as a straight border, in a circle or separated into individual motifs, to be enlarged or reduced as required. I am sure you will be excited by the versatility of this basic motif and see how easily it can be adapted to suit your own tastes and needs. This particular collection, for example, would look totally different yet equally effective if worked in subtle, smoky 'old-fashioned' colours such as peach, lavender and sage.

Gardens are many things – bright yet subdued, decorative yet functional, busy yet restful. Using them as inspiration and experimenting with size, colour and shape yields, as you will see, a rich harvest.

SPRING ANEMONE CUSHION

*A CIRCULAR GARLAND OF luscious anemones has been worked into this beautiful
cushion, although the design would look equally stunning if mounted
and framed as a wall picture. For an even more dramatic effect you could change
the colours to the gorgeous mauves, purples and inky-blues for which
the anemone is so well loved.*

MATERIALS

White Aida fabric (Zweigart E3706), 14-count, 20in (50cm)
   square
Printed cotton fabric suitable for the back of the cushion,
   16in (40cm) square
2 pieces of white cotton backing fabric, each 16in (40cm)
   square
DMC stranded cotton (floss): 2 skeins each Green 943,
   3345; 1 skein each Green 906; Red 891, 915; Pink 335,
   776; Mauve 553, 603, 3609; Blue 336; Black 310;
   Cream 746
White sewing thread
DMC coton perlé No 5 thread: 1 skein each Red 891;
   Green 943
Sewing thread to match either of the coton perlé threads
Cushion pad, 15in (38cm) square
Wooden frame, 17in (43cm) square

TO MAKE THE CUSHION

1 Stretch the Aida fabric carefully onto the frame, ensuring the straight grain is parallel to the sides of the frame.

2 Find the centre of the fabric by counting the sets of threads. Using the white sewing thread mark with tacking (basting) stitches the horizontal and vertical guidelines and so establish the centre of the fabric. This will also divide it into the four quarter sections.
NOTE: With this design the guidelines intersect in the centre of the fabric to give a central 'hole' rather than a central group of threads or cross stitch.

3 Use three strands of thread at all times. As always make sure that all upper stitches of the cross stitches face the same way to produce an even effect.

4 Carefully count outwards from the centre along one of the guidelines to locate where you wish to commence stitching. Always remember to fasten your threads securely on the wrong side and do not jump across the wrong side of the fabric from one area to another without finishing off the thread and starting afresh. This will conserve your thread and give a neater wrong side to your embroidery.

5 Continue working around the design, gradually building it up to form a circular garland of flowers and foliage.

6 When you work the simple border pattern that frames the inner garland you must repeat the four flower colours regularly around the square. The colour sequence will be continuous around the border pattern.

7 Once the design is complete remove the fabric carefully from the frame. Accurately count twenty-four sets of threads (or squares) out from the outer edge of the simple cross stitch border pattern to establish the seam line. Then count a further six sets of threads and mark this point temporarily with a dressmaker's pin. Cut along this line on each edge of the embroidered fabric.

8 Place one of the white fabric squares under the wrong side of the embroidered fabric. Join the layers by accurately machine straight stitching around the edges of the fabric on the seam line (twenty-four sets of threads from the edge of your cross stitch border).

9 To make up the cushion place the remaining white fabric square under the wrong side of the print cotton fabric square. Then with right sides together place the embroidered fabric over the print fabric. Pin, tack (baste) and machine straight stitch accurately along the seam line. Remember to leave a gap of approximately 9in (23cm) along one side for the insertion of the cushion pad.

10 Trim the layers of fabric across the corners of the seam allowance and turn the cushion to the right side. If necessary press the cover gently on the wrong side with a steam iron to remove any creases.

11 Place the cushion pad inside the cover and close the opening with neat and tiny slip stitches.

12 Make two equal lengths of twisted cord using the red and green coton perlé thread. For each cord cut four lengths of green and four of red thread all measuring 43in (110cm) (see Basic Stitches & Techniques, page 14). With matching sewing thread, hand stitch the cords around the cushion. You will find each cord will reach around two sides of the cushion. To finish, knot the loose ends of the cords, tease out these ends and trim to make mock tassels.

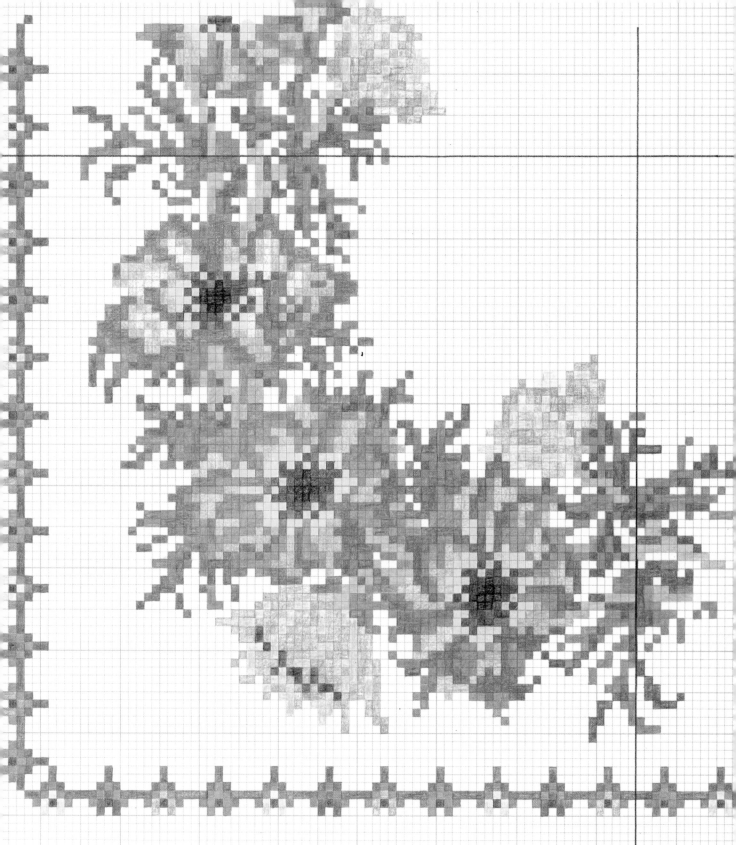

SPRING ANEMONE CUSHION

DMC STRANDED COTTON

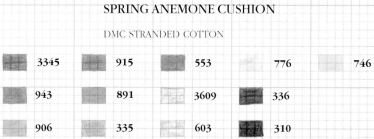

3345	915	553	776	746
943	891	3609	336	
906	335	603	310	

SCENTED SACHETS

*H*ERE ARE TWO DELIGHTFUL *ideas for making scented sachets. The square sachet is richly embellished, the vibrant flowers nestling within a square of the stylised border. The simple sachet is more subtle with just two bands of the stylised anemone flower border to decorate it. Neither sachet took very long to make and as gifts they would both be received with delight.*

SQUARE SACHET

MATERIALS

White Aida fabric (Zweigart E3706), 14-count, 10in (25cm) square

Printed cotton fabric suitable for back of sachet, 5½in (14cm) square

2 pieces of white cotton backing fabric, each 5½in (14cm) square

DMC stranded cotton (floss): 1 skein each Green 906, 943, 3345; Red 891, 915; Pink 335, 776; Mauve 553, 603, 3609; Blue 336; Black 310; Cream 746

White sewing thread

Small amount of Terylene or polyester filling

Small amount of pot-pourri

DMC coton perlé No 5 thread: 1 skein each Red 891; Green 943

Sewing thread to match either coton perlé threads

Wooden frame, 8in (20cm) square or wooden embroidery hoop, 8in (20cm) in diameter

TO MAKE THE SQUARE SACHET

1 Mount the Aida fabric on the frame or within the hoop ensuring the grain of the fabric is straight.

2 Find the centre of the fabric by counting the sets of threads and mark with a dressmaker's pin.

3 Use three strands of thread at all times and starting in the centre of the design (removing the pin first), follow the chart until your design is complete.

4 Remove the fabric from the frame or hoop. You may need to press the fabric on the wrong side with a steam iron.

5 Trim away the excess fabric leaving a 5½in (14cm) square of fabric. Use the grain of the fabric to ensure your design is positioned centrally within the square.

6 With right sides together pin the embroidered Aida fabric and one of the white cotton squares together, leaving a ⅜in (1cm) seam allowance on each edge. Using white sewing thread machine straight stitch these pieces together.

7 With right sides together place the print fabric square on top of the embroidered (and now backed) square. Then place the remaining white backing square on top of the print fabric. Tack (baste) and machine straight stitch the layers together following the line of stitching that you have already worked. Remember to leave an opening of approximately 2¼in (5.5cm) along one side.

8 Carefully trim the surplus fabric across the corners of the seam allowance and turn the sachet to the right side and press gently with a steam iron on the wrong side if necessary.

9 Place the polyester or Terylene filling inside the sachet adding some pot-pourri at the same time. Turn in the raw edges of the opening and neatly slip stitch close the opening.

10 Cut four lengths of green and four of red coton perlé thread each measuring 39in (1m). Use them to make a two-colour twisted cord (see Basic Stitches and Techniques, page 14). Then with matching sewing thread hand stitch the cord around the sachet. Knot ends of cord and tease and trim them to make mock tassels. Arrange and stitch the cords into a bow.

SCENTED SQUARE SACHET

DMC STRANDED COTTON

	3345		915		553		776		746
	943		891		3609		336		
	906		335		603		310		

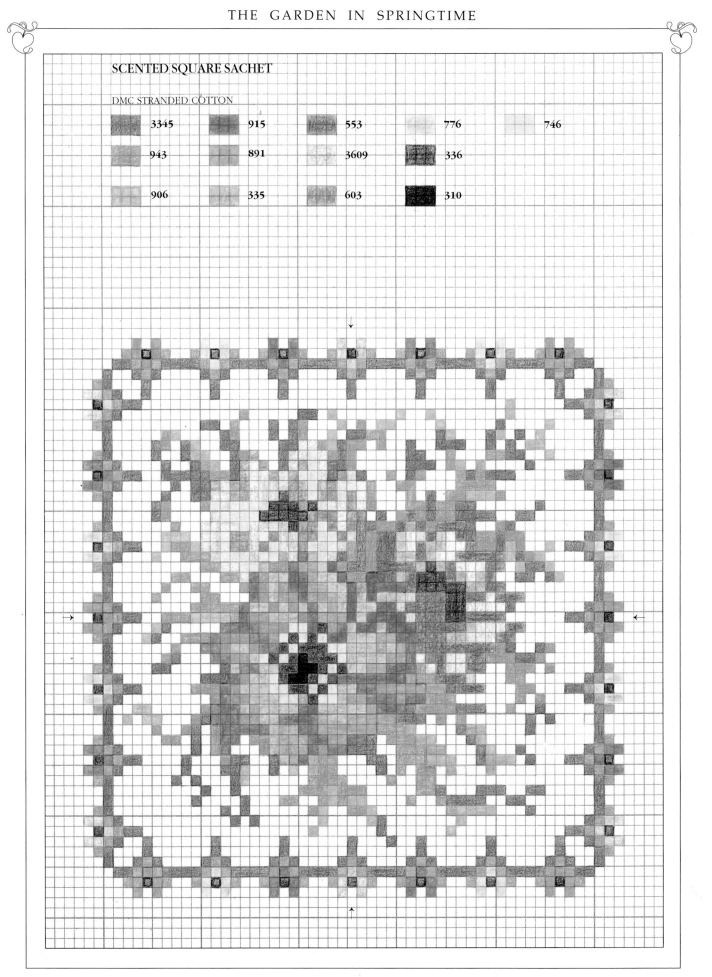

SIMPLE SACHET

MATERIALS
White Aida fabric (Zweigart E3706), 14-count, 7¼in
 (18.5cm) square
DMC stranded cotton (floss): small amounts of Green 943,
 3345; Red 891, 915; Pink 776; Mauve 3609; Blue 336
DMC coton perlé No 5 thread: small amounts of Red 891;
 Green 943
White sewing thread
Small amount of Terylene or polyester filling
Small amount of pot-pourri

TO MAKE THE SIMPLE SACHET

1 It is probably easier to work the simple border patterns without a frame but take care to keep an even tension. Work a row of the pattern 1¼in (3cm) away from one edge of the fabric. Then work a second line along the opposite edge, 3½in (9cm) away from the first row.

2 When completed, press the work on the wrong side.

3 If your sewing machine has an embroidery stitch facility select a scallop edge or any suitable edging stitch. Using white sewing thread work along the edge of the second border pattern positioning your line of machine stitching approximately ¾in (2cm) away. Trim away the excess fabric to give a decorative edge.

4 With right sides together fold the unworked edges together, then with a ⅜in (1cm) allowance, work a machine straight stitch seam along this edge.

5 Fold and flatten the tube of fabric so that the seam lies in the middle and at the back of the sachet. With the same seam allowance work a line of machine straight stitch across the bottom edge of the sachet.

6 Turn the sachet to the right side and place a little of your chosen filling and pot-pourri inside the bag. Only fill to approximately ¾in (2cm) below the upper border pattern.

7 Cut four lengths of red and four of green coton perlé thread each measuring 31½in (80cm). Use them to make a two-colour twisted cord (see Basic Stitches and Techniques, page 14). Knot the cord and tease out the loose ends of thread to make tassels. Tightly tie the cord around the sachet to hold the filling and pot-pourri securely. Tie a neat bow to complete this delightfully simple sachet.

TOWEL BORDER

A REPEATING BORDER PATTERN of the bright anemone motif decorates this guest towel (see page 23) but the design could easily be lengthened to fit a larger towel.

MATERIALS

White guest towel, 16in (40cm) wide

White Aida fabric (Zweigart E3706), 14-count, 8 x 22in (20 x 56cm)

DMC stranded cotton (floss): 2 skeins each Green 943, 3345; 1 skein each Green 906; Red 891, 915; Pink 335, 776; Mauve 553, 603, 3609; Blue 336; Black 310; Cream 746

White sewing thread

Small rotating frame, or wooden embroidery hoop, 6in (15cm) in diameter

TO MAKE THE TOWEL BORDER

1 If you are using a rotating frame mount the short ends of the Aida on the rotating sides and roll the excess fabric around one of these sides. If using a hoop place one end of the strip within the hoop, re-positioning as you work along the border.

2 Find the centre of the width of the fabric by counting the sets of threads and mark it temporarily with a dressmaker's pin – this will help you position your cross stitch border design centrally along the strip of fabric.

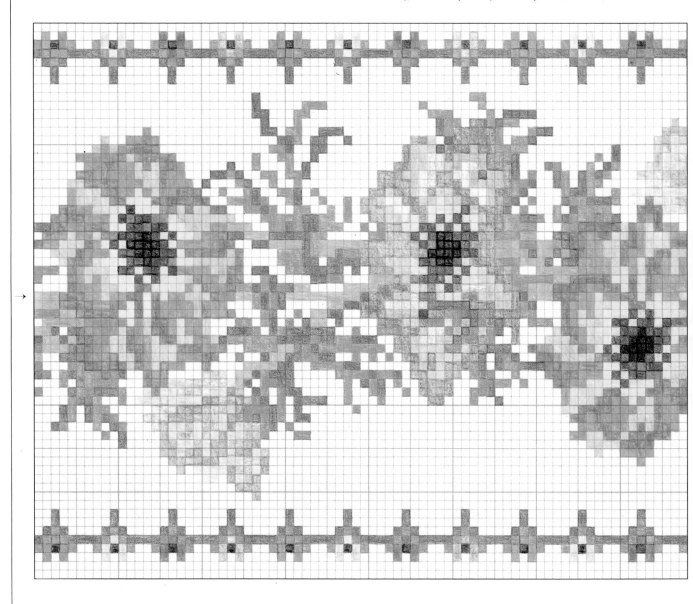

3 Use three strands of thread at all times. Remember to work your cross stitches so that all the upper stitches face the same way to produce an even effect.

4 The border design is a simple repeat pattern of a small spray of anemone flowers which have been reversed and then alternated. The stylised design along each edge of the border strip is worked continuously along the fabric repeating the four different flower colours as necessary.

5 Work along the length of the strip, repeating the design just over twice for the width of the guest towel. When nearing the end of the strip, measure the exact width of the towel and work the border to fit this measurement.

6 Remove the fabric from the frame or hoop and press it carefully on the wrong side, using a steam iron. This will encourage the stitchery to stand out on the right side.

7 With the cross stitch border centrally positioned cut away the surplus fabric at either side to give a strip which is 5in (13cm) wide. Similarly trim the surplus fabric at the ends of the border, leaving ⅜in (1cm) at each end for a small turning.

8 Pin and tack (baste) the border across one end of the towel, tucking in the turned allowance at both ends. With white sewing thread, machine satin stitch along the raw edges of the border, covering them completely with the width of the satin stitch and attaching the strip to the towel securely.

9 Finally, slip stitch the turned allowances to the towel sides to complete your guest towel.

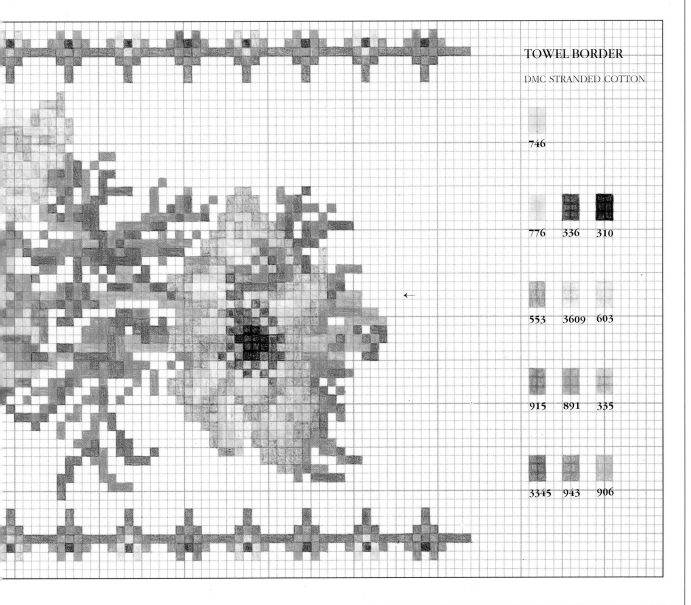

TOWEL BORDER

DMC STRANDED COTTON

746		
776	336	310
553	3609	603
915	891	335
3345	943	906

CHAPTER 2

The Bountiful Garden

I HAVE ALWAYS FOUND the sight of orderly rows of vegetables growing healthily in their allotted space in a garden to be both evocative and inspirational. Memories of visits to relatives and their gardens in the country still evoke images of Beatrix Potter-like scenes and it was with these ideas in mind that I designed The Bountiful Garden collection.

Vegetable growing is a passion with many people and I found designing cross stitch vegetable motifs to be addictive too – so many delicious ones to choose from. In the end I selected carrots, onions, cauliflowers and tomatoes as I liked their colours and shapes and felt they would look good together in a series of uncomplicated designs. In fact their warm, inviting tones and realistic shapes make the finished designs seem almost edible!

The main motifs are simple and uncluttered but well-balanced with a touch of humour, creating a fresh and unusual combination of shapes and colours. The framed vegetable pictures in particular were great fun to do – ideal to decorate the kitchen or dining room walls or to give as gifts. Other projects adapted from the main design include gift cards and tags, towel borders and a place mat and matching napkin that will give guests a healthy appetite even before the food is served!

FOUR FRAMED VEGETABLE PICTURES

THIS CHARMING SET OF four wall pictures (see page 26) will bring a smile to any onlooker's face. The naive three-dimensional soft vegetables at each corner add something special to these simple designs. However, if you do not want to spend time making these tiny vegetables then do not worry, the designs are equally effective without them and would perhaps look more sophisticated.

MATERIALS

Cream 264, Aida fabric (Zweigart E3706), 14-count , four pieces each measuring 11in (28cm) square

DMC stranded cotton (floss): 3 skeins Green 581, 991, 3819; 1 skein each Cream 746; Pale Yellow 745; Grey 3024; Red 347; Orange 740, 900; Brown 611, 738, 977

Small scraps of orange, red, bright green and various shades of dark green felt

Orange, red and green sewing thread

Very small amount of polyester or Terylene filling

Strong buttonhole thread (any colour)

Firm mounting cardboard cut to give four pieces each 6½in (16cm) square

4 wooden frames each measuring 7½in (19cm) square (without glass) with 5½in (14cm) square aperture

Strong, clear glue suitable for use with fabric

Wooden rectangular frame 9in (23cm) square (or other suitable frame of your choice)

TO MAKE THE VEGETABLE PICTURES

1 The four pictures are all worked in the same way. Start by stretching one piece of the Aida over the frame, ensuring the grain is straight and parallel to the sides.

2 Find, and temporarily mark with tacking (basting) stitches, the centre hole of the fabric.

3 Use three strands of embroidery thread at all times. Follow your chosen chart working all the cross stitches neatly and facing the same way. Once complete remove the tacking (basting) stitches and take off the frame.

4 Trim 1¼in (3cm) away from the sides of the fabric. If necessary press on the wrong side with an iron.

5 Use strong buttonhole thread to lace the fabric centrally over one square of mounting cardboard (see Basic Stitches

and Techniques, page 15). Now place the stretched embroidery within the purchased wooden frame.

6 Repeat steps 1–5 with the three remaining designs.

Now you can decide whether or not to add the delightful little three-dimensional vegetables around your framed designs. I chose to make a selection of tomatoes, carrots and cauliflowers as these shapes worked well together and were easy to make. Use the templates on page 30.

TO MAKE THE CARROTS

1 Cut out sixteen carrot shapes from the scraps of orange felt. The template is to be used as a guide. You can vary the size of it a little to make smaller carrots but avoid enlarging them as they could become too big and possibly dominate the design.

2 Fold one felt shape in half lengthwise. Use orange sewing thread to oversew (with tiny stitches) the straight sides together. Start at the pointed end and work towards the wider end. When you reach the curved top of the carrot work a row of very small running stitches around the edge.

3 Stuff the carrot shape with a small amount of filling. Do not pull the sewing thread up tightly yet.

4 Cut four lengths of either light or medium green stranded embroidery thread each measuring approximately 2in (5cm) long. Tie the lengths together centrally and then fold them in half at the knot so that you can push the knotted end into the top of the felt carrot. Now pull the gathering thread tightly to draw the felt up and around the green tuft of threads. Work several stitches backwards and forwards through the top of the carrot to hold the tuft in place and secure the gathering stitches.

5 Repeat steps 1–4 to make fifteen more carrots.

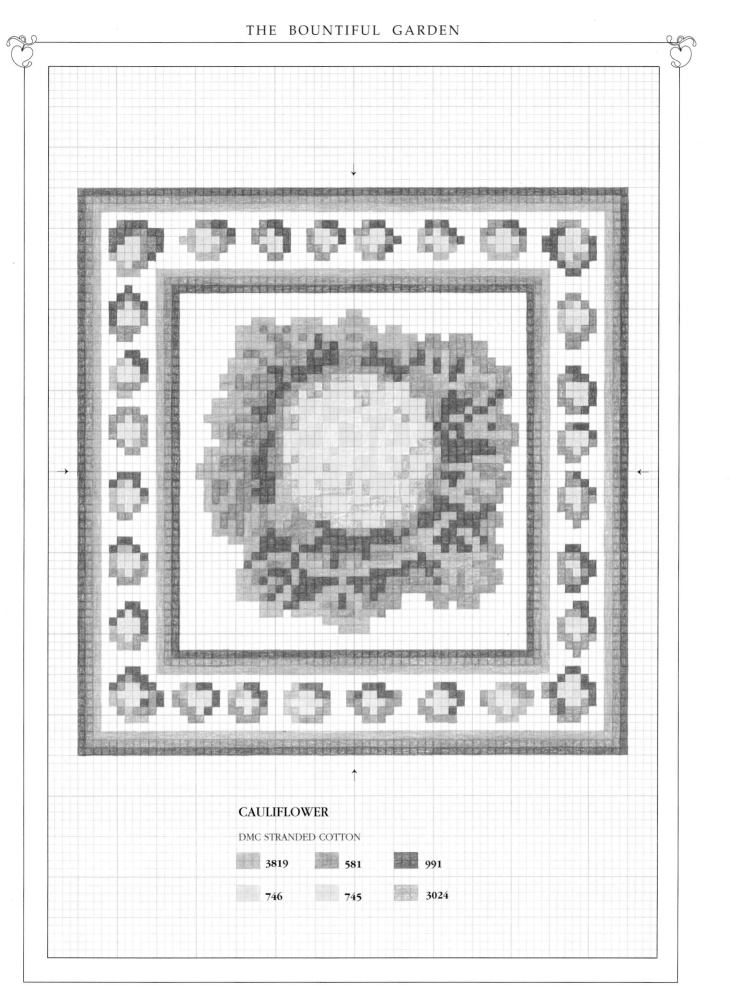

CAULIFLOWER

DMC STRANDED COTTON

3819	581	991
746	745	3024

TO MAKE THE TOMATOES

1 Cut out sixteen tomato shapes from the scraps of red, orange and bright green felt. As with the carrots use the template as a guide and make some of the tomatoes smaller by cutting some circles smaller than the template.

2 With matching sewing thread work a line of small running stitches around the edge of one of the felt circles. Gently pull the thread to gather the fabric a little. Stuff the tomato with a very small amount of filling and then pull the gathering thread as tightly as you can before working several oversewing stitches to secure the gathering.

3 On the smooth side of the tomato work five small straight stitches using six strands of dark green cotton, radiating the stitches from one point. In the centre of these stitches work a single French knot. Take the needle and thread through to the wrong side of the tomato and work a few oversewing stitches to secure the thread. Then pass the needle back through the tomato and the French knot before cutting the thread, leaving a short amount of thread as a stalk.

4 Repeat steps 1–3 to make fifteen more tomatoes in a variety of colours to represent stages of ripening and add interest to your design.

TO MAKE THE CAULIFLOWERS

1 Cut out sixteen large cauliflower shapes and sixteen small shapes using a variety of dark green scraps of felt. Once more, your cut shapes can vary a little from the templates shown here.

2 Place one small leaf shape centrally over one large shape. With dark green sewing thread work a line of small running stitches around the centre of the leaf shape, (making sure you stitch through both layers of felt. Gently pull the sewing thread to gather the fabric and produce the leaves of the cauliflower.

3 Use six strands of either cream or pale yellow embroidery cotton (floss) to work a dense cluster of French knots in the centre of the leaf circle. You will probably need to work approximately fifteen French knots to produce the desired effect.

4 Repeat steps 1–3 to make fifteen more cauliflowers.

ATTACHING THE VEGETABLES TO THE FRAMES

Use the photograph on pages 26–7 to help you arrange the vegetables around each picture. When you are satisfied carefully glue them into place.

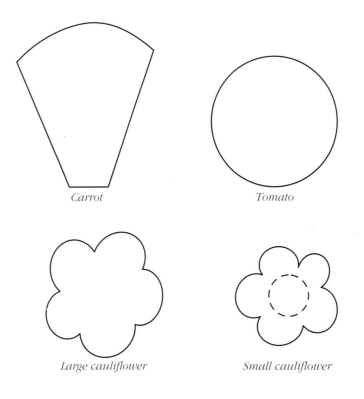

Carrot

Tomato

Large cauliflower

Small cauliflower

Templates for the three-dimensional vegetables

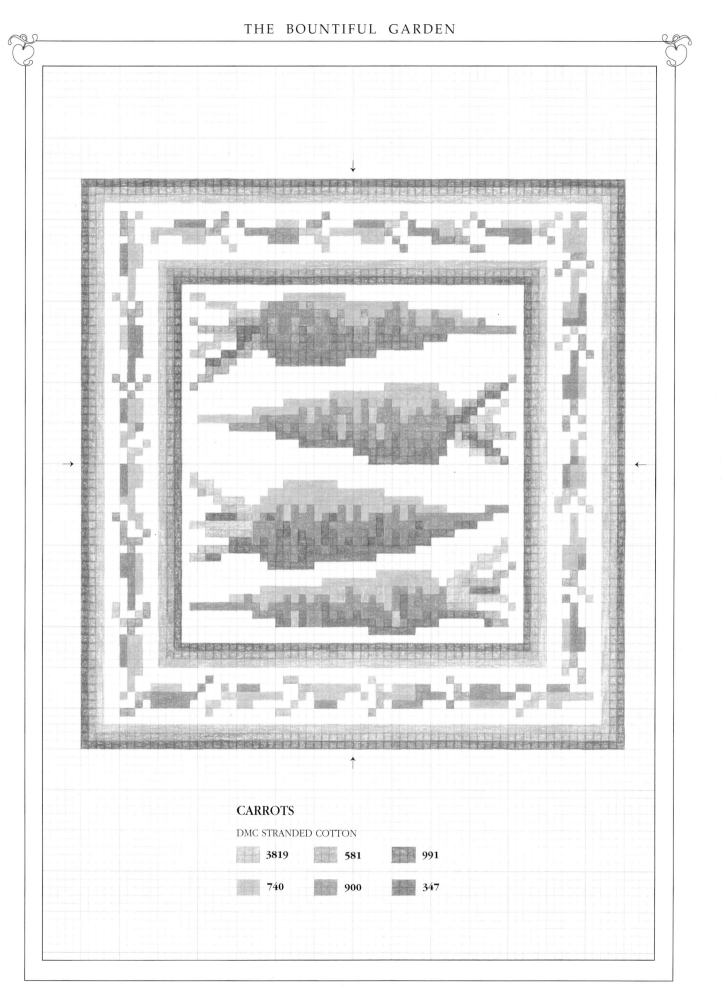

CARROTS

DMC STRANDED COTTON

3819   581   991

740   900   347

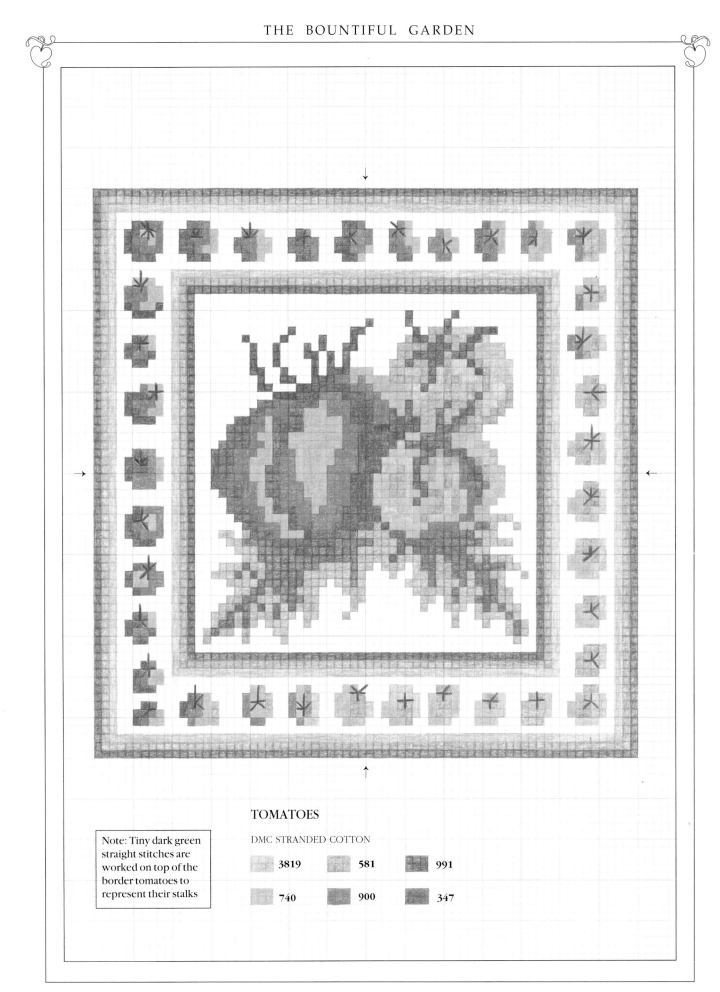

Note: Tiny dark green straight stitches are worked on top of the border tomatoes to represent their stalks

TOMATOES

DMC STRANDED COTTON

3819	581	991
740	900	347

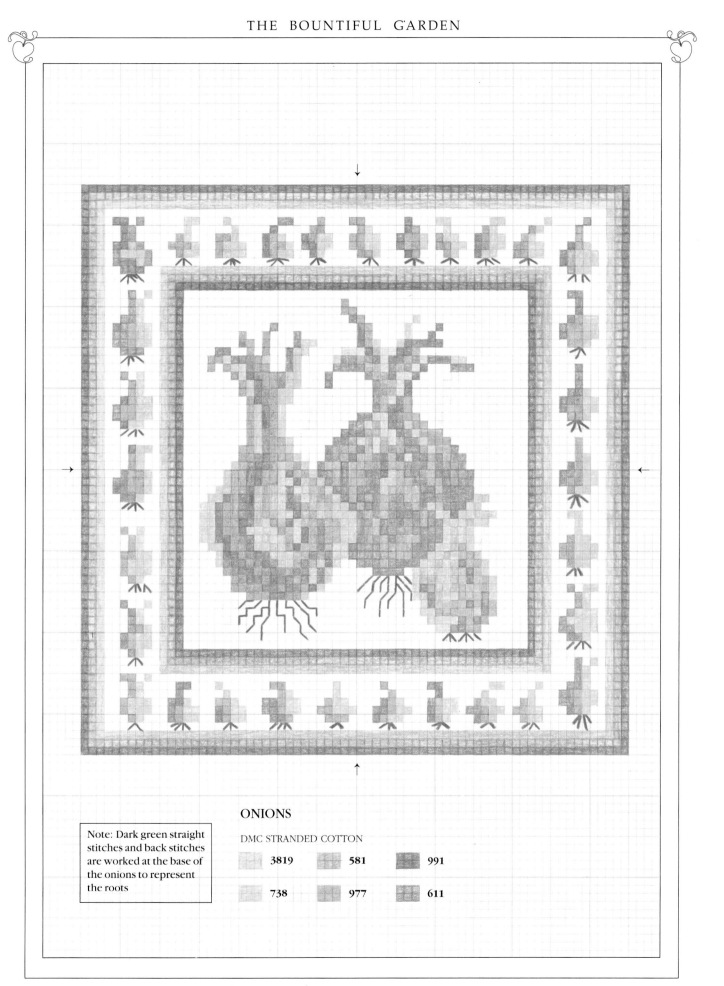

ONIONS

DMC STRANDED COTTON

3819		581		991	
738		977		611	

Note: Dark green straight stitches and back stitches are worked at the base of the onions to represent the roots

GIFT CARDS & TAGS

*A HAND-MADE CARD or tag will always make the smallest gift seem special,
particularly as the card can then be framed to become an everlasting
memory. This selection has been made using only small amounts of fabric
and thread and only took a short time to make.*

MATERIALS

White or cream window gift cards and gift tags, (window
for card measures 2½in (6.5cm) diameter, window for
tag measures 1¼in (3cm) diameter

Small pieces of Cream 264, Aida fabric (Zweigart E3706),
14-count, (larger than the windows of your cards and tags)

DMC stranded cotton (floss): small amounts of Green 581,
991, 3819; Cream 746; Pale Yellow 745; Grey 3024; Red 347;
Orange 740, 900; Brown 611, 738, 977

Strong, clear glue suitable for fabric and card

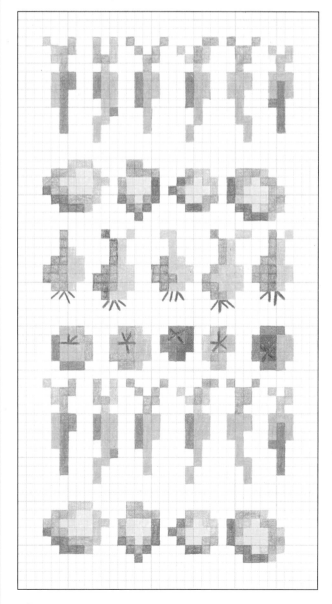

TO MAKE THE GIFT CARDS AND TAGS

This project is so simple and adaptable that you can make
any number of charming variations and combinations.
Depending on the size of your fabric you can either work
the embroidery in a small hoop or freely in your hand.
The tags require such a small amount of fabric that this
project provides the ideal opportunity to use up small
scraps of expensive Aida fabric from larger projects.

The chart here (with its key on page 36) shows the
rows of vegetables as they appear on the larger gift cards.
I simply worked the top three rows for one card and
three more rows for the second card. If the windows of
your cards are a different size to those used here you can
quite easily work your rows of vegetables to fit the window. Similarly the gift tags are very easily worked, simply
by grouping a few vegetables together.

Remember, if you are worried about your embroidery
fitting the window it is easy for you to check by opening
out the card or tag and placing the window area over
your stitchery.

1 Use three strands of embroidery thread at all times.
Work the designs making sure all the cross stitches face
the same way. The tiny tomatoes all have four or five
small straight stitches worked freely on them to represent
the stalks. Similarly the short roots of the onions are
worked in the same way.

2 Press your finished embroidery on the wrong side
with a steam iron if necessary to remove any creases.

3 Assemble the gift cards and tags. Open out one card
and place the embroidered fabric in the correct position
over the window section. Measure and trim away any
excess fabric so that your fabric is ⅜in (1cm) bigger all
round than the window shape (or slightly less with the
tags).

4 Carefully glue the fabric in place behind the window
mount. Then glue the left-hand section of the gift card to
the back of the embroidery in the window section.

Repeat this process with the gift tags. You may have to
trim away a little more fabric around the edges of the
embroidery depending on the size of the tag.

*The lines of vegetables can be repeated vertically and
horizontally. The chart key is on page 36*

TOWEL SET

I HAVE WORKED A cauliflower border for a guest towel and a carrot border for the larger hand towel. Both borders are simple and grow quickly. As with the rest of this collection they use a small amount of materials. You can purchase ready-made border strips by the yard; however, I chose to use the same Aida fabric as for the pictures, cards and tags.

MATERIALS

Cream towels, guest towel approximately 16in (40cm) wide, hand towel approximately 20in (50cm) wide

Cream 264, Aida fabric (Zweigart E3706), 14-count, 6½ x 24in (16 x 60cm) if working the two borders together on one strip of fabric, or 4 x 20in (10 x 50cm) for guest towel and 4 x 24in (10 x 60cm) for hand towel

DMC stranded cotton (floss): 1 skein each Green 581, 991, 3819; Red 347; Orange 740, 900; Cream 746; Pale Yellow 745; Grey 3024

Cream sewing thread to match Aida fabric and towels

Small rotating frame

NOTE: If you do not have a small rotating frame you can work these border strips in a tiny hoop but you will have to repeatedly re-position the hoop and risk marking the fabric. Alternatively you can work the strips freely in your hands but do take extra care with the tension of your stitchery.

TO MAKE THE TOWEL BORDERS

1 Stretch and fix the short ends of the Aida fabric centrally to the rotating sides of the frame. For speed I simply staple the fabric to the wooden rollers, using a staple gun.

2 Roll the excess fabric around one of the rollers to produce an area that is quite taut even though the other two sides are not fixed to the frame sides.

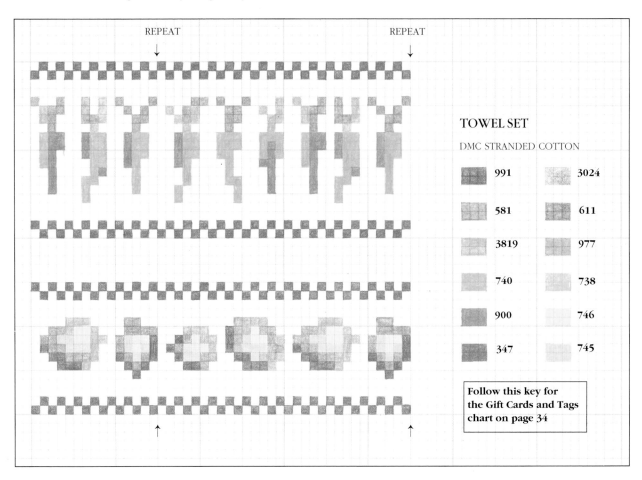

REPEAT

REPEAT

TOWEL SET

DMC STRANDED COTTON

	991		3024
	581		611
	3819		977
	740		738
	900		746
	347		745

Follow this key for the Gift Cards and Tags chart on page 34

Although I have only used carrots and cauliflowers to create the border designs you could easily adapt the idea to use the onions and tomatoes or even a mixture of all four vegetables

3 At the beginning of the strip carefully count across the width to find the centre hole. Mark this with a pin and then count twenty holes back from the centre on either side to establish the centre holes of each border strip. You may wish to tack (baste) along these two lines and use them as guide lines while you are beginning the embroidery. If you are working the two strips separately them simply find the centre of the width of each strip before commencing the stitchery.

4 Use three strands of embroidery thread at all times and make sure all your cross stitches are worked to face the same way. Follow the chart on page 36 to work a row of carrots centring them along one of your guidelines. Similarly work a line of cauliflowers centrally along the other guideline. For the cauliflower guest towel your border will need to measure 16¼in (41cm) and for the carrot hand towel the border will need to measure 20¼in (51cm).

5 Work the dark green edging to complete your border strips. Check each border is the correct length.

6 Remove the fabric from the frame. If necessary press the fabric on the wrong side with a steam iron.

7 Starting from the outermost line of stitching along each border edge, count and mark the fourth hole and with sharp scissors very carefully cut away the excess fabric leaving the border strip ready to be attached to the towel.

8 Pin and tack (baste) the Aida strip across the woven band of one end of the towel. Trim across the short ends of the strip leaving a ⅜in (1cm) turning allowance. Tuck this allowance between the border and the towel. With cream sewing thread, machine satin stitch along the raw edges of the border, covering them with the width of the satin stitching. This line of stitching will prevent the Aida fabric from fraying and also neatly and securely attach it to the towel.

9 Finally, slip stitch the turned allowances to the sides of the towel to complete.

PLACE MAT & NAPKIN

THIS DELIGHTFUL PLACE MAT and matching napkin set took only a little longer to make than the gift cards on pages 34–5. The place mat and napkin are purchased ready-made and are made of wonderful natural fibres just right for this project. I have simply worked three rows of the tiny vegetables on page 34 and then mounted them on the mat and napkin. If you wish you can work more or less of the rows. You could even make charming napkin rings to match.

MATERIALS
Fabric and threads as for gift cards (see page 34)
Cream cotton place mat and matching napkin

TO MAKE THE PLACE MAT AND NAPKIN

1 Select and work your rows of vegetables as for the gift cards. You can see in the photograph that I have worked a row of five onions above five tomatoes, above six carrots, but you may wish to select a different combination.

2 When you have completed your rows of vegetables press the fabric gently on the wrong side with a steam iron and then carefully trim away the excess fabric leaving five sets of threads around each side of your stitched design (count from the outermost stitches on each side of the design). Use very sharp trimming scissors and make sure you cut the fabric straight along the rows of holes and not through the groups of threads.

3 Pin the embroidered fabric in the desired position on your place mat and napkin (I chose the top right corners), aligning the edges of the Aida fabric with the edges of the place mat and napkin.

4 Using dark green embroidery thread work a border around the rows of vegetables to match the border on the towels (see page 36). Position the border one square away from the vegetables and one square in from the cut edge. Work through both layers of fabric neatly and evenly so that while you are creating the border pattern around these delightful designs you are also firmly attaching the Aida fabric to the mat or napkin fabric.

5 Finally, using a pin tease away the outer group of threads from the edges of the Aida fabric to complete your place set.

CHAPTER 3

The Summer Garden

THERE ARE FEW PLANTS *more evocative of summer than roses – perfect roses in gorgeous colours, full-blooms heavy with scent, tight buds promising more. With strong images of pinks, salmons and yellows, simple old-fashioned roses and hot summery days passing through my mind I set about designing this collection of embroidery when the weather was cold and grey. Working these delightful designs brought much enjoyment to me and helped bring the summer days closer.*

The cushion design was my starting point for all the other projects in the chapter. Its lush circular garland of roses led on to a charming little scented sachet filled with rose-scented pot-pourri, an elegant place mat and napkin holder set edged with a rose border, two useful trinket boxes, their lids decorated with simple rose designs and some rose motif gift cards. The great variety of designs are there for you to recreate or, better still, adapt into ideas of your own.

SUMMER ROSES CUSHION

THIS LOVELY CUSHION HAS an outer garland of beautiful pastel roses with full blooms, tiny buds and hips – it even has bumble bees hovering around it and a suggestion of tiny ladybirds amongst the leaves. The centre section of the cushion is more stylised and doubles to make a charming design for the scented sachet.

MATERIALS

Sage 611 Aida fabric (Zweigart E3706), 14-count, 20in (50cm) square

Sage-green fabric suitable for the back of the cushion, 16in (40cm) square (I used a lightweight brocade furnishing fabric)

White cotton backing fabric, two pieces, each 16in (40cm) square

DMC stranded cotton (floss): 3 skeins Green 3814; 2 skeins each Green 367, 580, 703; 1 skein each Green 471; Red 350; Pink 948, 3733; Yellow 725, 744; Salmon 3825; Brown 610, 3045

DMC coton perlé No5 thread, 2 skeins Green 992

Sewing thread to match fabric

Cushion pad, 15in (38cm) square

Wooden embroidery frame, 17in (43cm) square

TO MAKE THE CUSHION

1 Stretch the Aida fabric onto the frame, ensuring the straight grain is parallel to the sides. Find and mark the centre hole of the fabric with tacking (basting) stitches.

2 Work the embroidery using three strands of thread at all times unless otherwise directed. Start by working the centre section and then moving outwards, building up the outer garland of roses. Ensure all cross stitches are constructed in the same way.

3 Work the antennae, legs and wings of the bees in back stitches (see Basic Stitches and Techniques page 13). The legs and antennae are worked in three strands of dark brown thread with the wings in only two strands of lighter brown to give a more delicate effect. When stitching the wings stitch *into* the sets of threads rather than always into the holes of the fabric (see chart on page 44). Finally, I added lots of clusters of tiny French knots (see Basic Stitches and Techniques page 14) around the centres of the open roses of the outer garland. I also added clusters of knots to the rose hips where the petals have fallen. These French knots raise the embroidery up and out of the fabric and give a delightful finishing touch.

4 To make up the cushion, remove the embroidered fabric from the frame. Accurately count twenty-four sets of threads (or squares) out from the outer edge of the green border pattern to establish the seam line. Now count a further six sets of threads and mark with a pin. Accurately cut along this line on all sides of the cushion to trim away the excess fabric.

5 Place one of the white fabric squares under the wrong side of the embroidered fabric. Join the layers by accurately machine straight stitching in green thread around the edges of the fabric on the seam line (twenty-four sets of threads away from the edge of the green border pattern).

6 Place the remaining white fabric square under the wrong side of the green backing fabric. (I added an extra layer of fabric to support my green brocade fabric but you may wish to omit it.) With right sides together place the embroidered fabric over the sage-green backing fabric. Pin, tack (baste) and machine straight stitch accurately along the seam line. Remember to leave a gap of approximately 10in (25cm) along one side.

7 Trim the layers of fabric across the corners of the seam allowance and turn to the right side. If necessary press the cover gently on the wrong side to remove creases. Place the cushion pad inside the cover and close the opening with tiny slip stitches.

8 Make a long twisted cord using the two skeins of green coton perlé thread. Carefully unravel each skein and divide them equally into four lengths per skein (eight lengths in total). Tie the threads together at the ends and make the twisted cord (see Basic Stitches and Techniques page 14). You will need to do this carefully and patiently as the length of cord can twist up on itself and appear muddled but with care you can make a long cord.

9 Hand stitch the cord around the seam line of the cushion. Allow about 5in (12cm) to hang loose at the start and leave the same amount when you reach this corner once more. Tie a knot in the cord before cutting off the excess and leave approximately ⅝in (1.5cm) of thread beyond the knot to make a mock tassel by teasing out the fibres of the threads with a pin. Trim to neaten. Make a mock tassel on the other loose end of the cord. Carefully arrange the loose ends of the cords at the corner to give the appearance of a bow and stitch in place to finish the cushion.

NOTE: Reserve the remaining length of twisted cord to decorate the Rose-scented Sachet (see page 45).

SUMMER ROSES CUSHION

DMC STRANDED COTTON

744	3825	948	3045	471	3814	580
725	350	3733	610	703	367	

ROSE-SCENTED SACHET

THIS CHARMING LITTLE SACHET, filled with rose-scented pot-pourri, uses the central design from the cushion, showing a bumble bee spoilt for choice by the many roses surrounding it. The sachet is quickly worked and uses only small amounts of materials. You could probably use left-over threads from the cushion.

MATERIALS

Sage 611 Aida fabric (Zweigart E3706), 14-count, 8in (20cm) square

Sage-green fabric suitable for the back of the sachet, 5½in (14cm) square

Two pieces white cotton backing fabric, each 5½in (14cm) square

DMC stranded cotton (floss): small amounts of Green 367, 580, 703, 3814; Red 350; Pink 948, 3733; Yellow 725; Salmon 3825; Brown 610, 3045

Green sewing thread to match fabric

DMC coton perlé No 5 thread, 1 skein Green 992 (use remainder from the cushion)

Sewing thread to match fabric

Small amount of rose-scented pot-pourri

Wooden embroidery hoop, 7in (18cm) diameter

TO MAKE THE ROSE-SCENTED SACHET

1 Mount the Aida fabric in the hoop ensuring the grain of the fabric is straight.

2 Find the centre hole of the fabric and mark with tacking (basting) stitches.

3 Use three strands of embroidery thread to work all the embroidery except for the delicate wings of the bumble bee (see Summer Roses Cushion, step 3, page 42).

4 When your embroidery is complete remove the fabric from the hoop and press it gently on the wrong side with a steam iron to remove any creases and enhance the stitchery.

5 Carefully count outwards from the corners (there will be two cross stitches side by side) to the tenth hole. Mark with a pin at each corner. Then using a ruler and a sharp-pointed crayon (similar in colour to the fabric) lightly draw a line from point to point around the small embroidered square. Leave a ⅜in (1cm) seam allowance beyond this line and cut away the excess fabric.

6 Trim the sage-green backing fabric to match the Aida fabric. Then with the right side uppermost place the embroidered square over one of the white lining squares and pin to hold. With green sewing thread, machine straight stitch accurately along the drawn straight lines.

7 With right sides together place the sage-green backing square over the embroidered square, and add the remaining white square on top. Pin and tack (baste) the layers together. Turn the layers over so that the stitched guide-lines are visible. Machine straight stitch around the sachet on the guidelines, remembering to leave one side open.

8 Trim away the excess fabric at the corners and turn to the right side.

9 Fill with pot-pourri, then turn in the raw edges of the open side and with matching thread slip stitch to close.

10 Use the green twisted cord left over from the cushion or make one using eight equal lengths of coton perlé thread 64in (160cm) long (see Basic Stitches and Techniques page 14).

With matching sewing thread hand stitch the cord around the sachet allowing for a loop of cord at the top corner. Neaten the loose ends of the cord at the lower corner and make mock tassels as for the cushion (see page 42).

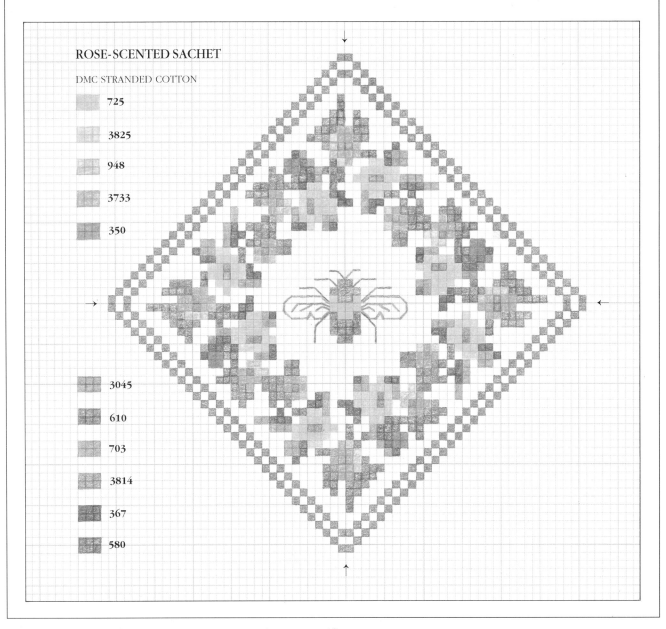

ROSE-SCENTED SACHET

DMC STRANDED COTTON

- 725
- 3825
- 948
- 3733
- 350
- 3045
- 610
- 703
- 3814
- 367
- 580

PLACE MAT & NAPKIN HOLDER

*T*HE SIMPLE FLOWER BUD *design in the centre section of the cushion design provided me with the inspiration for the border repeat pattern which I have used to decorate this elegant place mat and the matching napkin holder. The embroidery is quick to work and you could easily make a complete set of table linen. The design would also look very effective upon towels, bed linen and curtains.*

MATERIALS

For one place mat and napkin set

Sage 611 Aida fabric (Zweigart E3706), 14-count; 12 x 16in
   (30 x 40cm)

Sage-green place mat 13½ x 17½in (34 x 44cm) and
   matching napkin

Sage-green fabric for back of napkin holder, 3¼ x 8¼in
   (8 x 21cm)

DMC stranded cotton (floss): 1 skein each Green 367, 580,
   703, 3814; Pink 948, 3733; Yellow 725; Salmon 3825;
   Brown 3045

DMC coton perlé No 5 thread, 1 skein Green 992

Sewing thread to match fabric

1 small clear plastic press-stud

Small rotating frame

TO MAKE THE PLACE MAT AND NAPKIN HOLDER

1 Mount the short ends of your Aida fabric on the rotating sides of the frame and roll the excess fabric around one of these sides.

2 Divide the fabric by tacking (basting) into three equal sections each 4in (10cm) across its width. This will enable you to work the two border strips of the place mat side by side and also have enough fabric to work the napkin holder strip along the third section.

3 Use three strands of embroidery thread at all times. Position each border pattern centrally within the area of fabric you have allotted for it. Start the repeat pattern at the top of the chart shown and work downwards. You will see that the chart shows that the design is repeated every forty squares or cross stitches. Repeat the design nearly five times for each border of the place mat. Work the borders to fit your place mat (sizes may vary slightly). The embroidered strip for the napkin holder is much shorter. I worked the border design along eighty-two squares (just two repeats of the pattern plus two more squares) and then worked the green border on either side continuing across the short ends to complete.

4 When your embroidery is complete carefully remove the fabric from the frame and divide it into the three strips. Reserve the shorter section for the napkin holder.

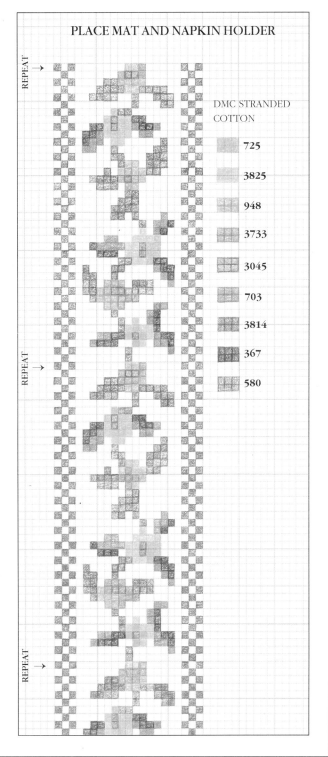

PLACE MAT AND NAPKIN HOLDER

REPEAT →

REPEAT →

REPEAT →

DMC STRANDED COTTON	
	725
	3825
	948
	3733
	3045
	703
	3814
	367
	580

5 Make up the place mat. Leaving four sets of threads on either side of the embroidered strips trim away the excess fabric. Similarly trim away the fabric at the ends of the strips. Remember to leave a small turning allowance at the ends.

6 Pin and tack (baste) the borders on the place mat in the desired position. (I positioned mine close to the ends of the place mat.) Then, with matching sewing thread, machine satin stitch along the raw edges of the borders, covering them completely with the width of the satin stitch and thus attaching the Aida strips to the place mat.

7 Finally, slip stitch the turned allowance neatly to the top and bottom edges of the mat.

8 To make the napkin holder, trim away the excess fabric around the embroidered strip leaving eight sets of threads on each side around the green border pattern. Then with right sides together place the embroidered strip centrally over the sage-green backing fabric. Pin to hold.

With the Aida fabric uppermost, count outwards from the edge of the green border, across four sets of threads. This will be the seam line. Machine straight stitch along this line with matching thread, leaving one of the short ends open. Clip across the seam allowance at the corners and carefully turn the fabric to the right side. If necessary press the fabric on the wrong side with a steam iron to remove any creases. Tuck in the seam allowance at the open short end and work small slip stitches to close.

9 Make a green twisted cord (see Basic Stitches and Techniques page 14) using four equal lengths of coton perlé thread, each measuring 2⅝yd (240cm).

10 Attach the twisted cord around the edges of the napkin holder starting and finishing in the centre of one of the shorter sides. Arrange the ends of the cord into a bow and stitch carefully into position. Make mock tassels at the raw ends of the cord.

11 Finally, stitch one half of the clear plastic press-stud on the wrong side of the napkin holder behind the cord bow and align the other half of the press-stud on the right side at the other end of the holder so that when the studs are pressed together the napkin holder forms a ring to hold the napkin.

TRINKET BOXES

THESE DELIGHTFUL PORCELAIN TRINKET boxes make wonderful gifts to family and friends. They are available in a variety of shapes, sizes and colours from good craft shops, are easy to put together and ideal for keeping all manner of items in. I felt that these particular ones were just waiting for some pretty cross stitch designs to be mounted in their lids.

MATERIALS

2 porcelain trinket boxes, DMC Creative World, Soft Green N850 1¼in (3cm) diameter and N851 2⅜in (6.5cm) diameter

Sage 611 Aida fabric (Zweigart E3706), 14-count, 8in (20cm) square

DMC stranded cotton (floss): small amounts of Green 367, 580, 703, 3814; Pink 948, 3733; Yellow 725; Salmon 3825; Brown 3045; Red 350

Wooden embroidery hoop, 7in (18cm) diameter

TO MAKE THE TRINKET BOXES

1 Place the fabric within the hoop ensuring the grain is straight. You can work both the designs within the hoop as there is plenty of fabric but do plan the positioning carefully, making sure there is approximately 1⅝in (4cm) between the outermost stitches of the designs to allow for cutting and mounting.

2 As before use three strands of embroidery thread at all times and work each of these tiny designs so that all the cross stitches are constructed in the same way.

3 When the stitching is complete remove the fabric from the frame and if necessary press it on the wrong side with a steam iron to remove any creases.

4 Following the manufacturer's instructions, mount the designs within the lids of the trinket boxes.

NOTE: I chose to mount my Summer Garden motifs in the lids without the use of the protective acetate circles over them, as I wanted the stitchery to stand out as much as possible. If you choose to do this remember that the fabric and threads will become dusty and a little soiled over time and that laundering is not possible.

To make use of some of the scraps of Aida fabric and the threads that are left over I have worked another of the larger circular motifs and mounted it within a blank gift card which are readily available from craft shops. This can be seen in the photograph on page 51.

Opposite: *Jewel-like circles of delicate yellow and pink miniature roses decorate these pretty trinket boxes and matching card*

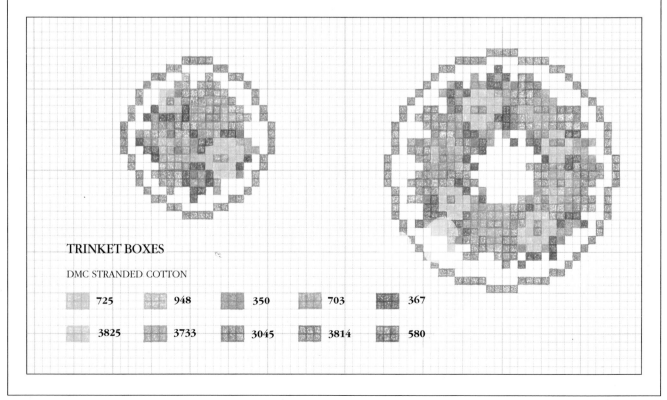

TRINKET BOXES

DMC STRANDED COTTON

	725		948		350		703		367
	3825		3733		3045		3814		580

CHAPTER 4

The Garden Collection

GARDENS FULFIL MANY DIFFERENT roles in our lives. They are the scene of ever-changing floral displays, and they provide a year-long harvest of fruit, vegetables and herbs.

The projects in this chapter reflect the versatility of our gardens. I have produced a set of deliberately naive, primitive designs that are similar in colouring and style to the work of artists such as Yugoslavian Ivan Rabuzin, showing just how effective this lively combination of the decorative and the utilitarian can be.

The basic motifs here are deceptively simple — rows of dipping, stylised washing lines decorate a pillowcase, duvet and cushion, while lines of flowerpots, top-heavy with blooms, stand to attention within the cushion design and also on the bath linen. A set of quickly worked floral pots and baskets have been framed and hung as wall pictures, but could also be made into special greetings cards.

Whether you long to see fat vegetables ripening in the summer sun, a rainbow display of flowers, a billowing line of freshly washed clothes, earthenware flowerpots clustered on a patio or all these elements together — the choice is yours.

WASHING LINES &
FLOWERPOTS CUSHION

THE STRONG, SKY-BLUE of the cushion fabric is one of my favourite colours. It is used here to set off the rainbow of colours used on the white Aida fabric. The effect is one of simple clarity so that the rows of clothes hanging from a washing line delights the eye as much as the pretty pot plants.

MATERIALS

White Aida fabric (Zweigart E3706), 14-count, 16in (40cm) square

DMC stranded cotton (floss): 2 skeins each Green 3348, 3816; Rust 356; 1 skein each Blue 800, 3807; Mauve 552, 3608; Pink 963; Yellow 745; Orange 742; Flesh 945

Deep sky-blue cotton fabric, 31in (80cm) of 48in (120cm) wide

White cotton backing fabric, 16in (40cm) square

Sewing thread, white and to match blue fabric

Cushion pad, 15in (38cm) square

DMC coton perlé No 5 thread: Green 992, Pink 605

Wooden frame, 15in (38cm) square

TO MAKE THE CUSHION

1 To work the embroidery, mount the white Aida fabric on your frame ensuring the fabric grain is parallel to the sides of the frame.

2 Find and mark with tacking (basting) stitches the centre stitch of the fabric.

3 Work the embroidery using three strands of thread at all times. You will find it beneficial to start by working the centre section completely and then working outwards, gradually building up the complete design. Ensure all your cross stitches are constructed in the same way to give a neat and even effect.

4 Once you have completed the stitchery remove the fabric from the frame.

5 To make the cushion, use ⅜in (1cm) seam allowance. Cut two strips across the width of the blue fabric, each measuring 8in (20cm) wide, 48in (120cm) long. From the remaining fabric cut two 16in (40cm) squares. Reserve the squares of fabric and use the strips to prepare the frill.

6 Join the two long strips together to form a continuous band. Fold the band in half lengthways to give a double thickness, 4in (10cm) wide. Press with an iron to neaten and give a crisp, folded edge. Along the double raw edge work two lines of gathering stitches either by hand or using a loose, machine straight stitch.

7 Place the white backing fabric square on a clean, flat surface, then place one of the blue cotton squares on top aligning the edges of the fabrics. Carefully trim excess Aida fabric from around the stitchery leaving two sets of Aida threads on all sides. Place your trimmed embroidered square centrally on top of the blue and white fabric squares. Pin and tack (baste) the layers together.

8 With your sewing machine set to a wide satin stitch use white thread to carefully attach the Aida fabric to the cotton fabrics. Work the line of stitching so that it covers the cut edge of the Aida.

9 Attach the frill to the cushion face. With right sides together and matching raw edges, pin the continuous band to the cushion face, drawing up the gathering threads gently, a little at a time so that the frill fits around the cushion. The frill is not extremely full so take care to ensure there are ample gathers at the corners to give a pleasing effect. With matching thread machine straight stitch the frill to the cushion face, working accurately along the seam line and taking care not to catch the folds of the frill at the corners.

10 With right sides facing, pin and tack (baste) the cushion back in position. Machine straight stitch along seam line, once more taking care not to catch the folds of the frill in line of stitching. Leave a gap in the seam of at least 8in (20cm) for inserting the cushion pad. Clip seam allowance and trim across corners. Gently turn cushion to the right side, trying not to crease fabric. Insert the cushion pad, then close the open seam with tiny slip stitches.

11 Make a long twisted cord using the two skeins of coton perlé thread (see Basic Stitches and Techniques page 14). Hand stitch the cord around the seam line of the cushion and frill. Allow 6in (15cm) to hang loose at the corner where you start stitching and the same amount when you reach this corner once more. Tie a knot in the cord before cutting off the excess and leave approximately ⅝in (1.5cm) of thread beyond the knot to make a mock tassel by teasing out the fibres of the threads with a pin. Trim tassel to neaten, then repeat at other end of the cord. Arrange cord into a bow and stitch in place.

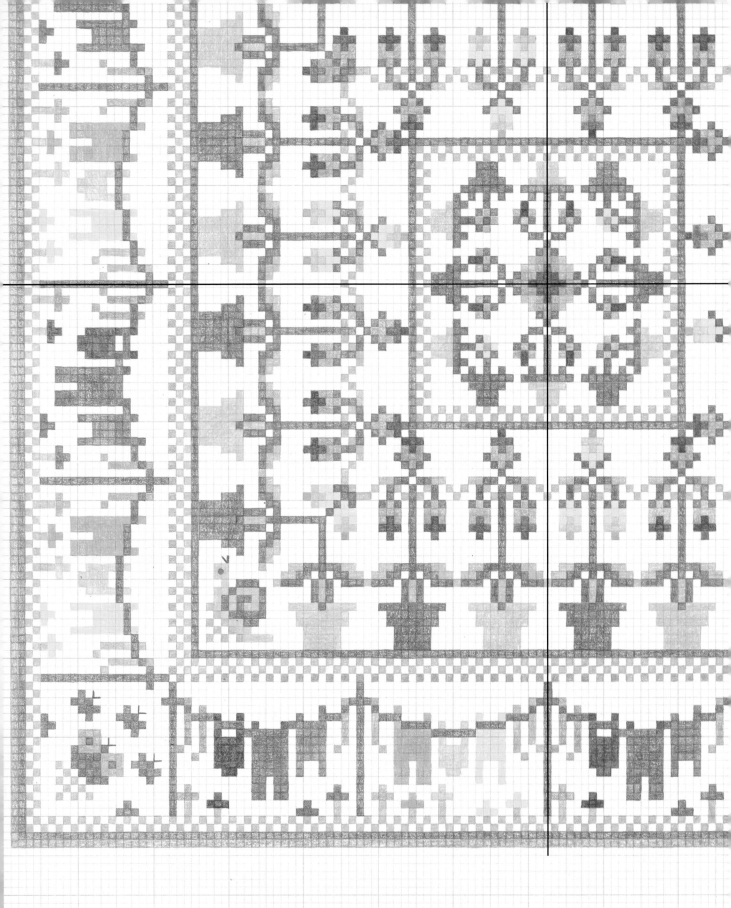

WASHING LINES & FLOWERPOTS CUSHION

DMC STRANDED COTTON

963		945		745		800	
3608		742		3348		3807	
552		356		3816			

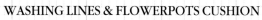

FLOWERPOTS BATH LINEN

Look carefully at the beautiful cushion design on page 55 and you will see rows of pot plants bordering the centre section of the design. I have extracted these charmingly simple motifs and repeated them to decorate the border strips of these hand and guest towels. I have used the same Aida fabric as the cushion but you may prefer to use an Aida band. These have neatened decorative edges in a variety of colours and widths. Zweigart's scalloped edge Aida band, Sky 151, E7107, 2in (5cm) wide would be suitable for the guest towel and E7195, 4in (10cm) wide for the hand towel. I used my small rotating frame to embroider the borders but it is possible to work them freely in the hand.

MATERIALS

White Aida fabric (Zweigart E3706), 14-count, 5 x 20in (13 x 50cm) for guest towel, 6 x 25in (15 x 64cm) for hand towel

DMC stranded cotton (floss): 2 skeins each Green 3348, 3816; 1 skein each Rust 356; Blue 800, 3807; Mauve 552, 3608; Pink 963; Yellow 745; Orange 742; Flesh 945

Deep sky-blue guest towel, 16in (40cm) wide

Deep sky-blue hand towel, 22in (56cm) wide

Sewing thread, white and deep sky-blue

Small rotating frame (optional)

TO MAKE THE GUEST TOWEL BORDER

1 Mount the ends of the Aida fabric on the rotating frame and roll the excess fabric onto one of the rollers.

2 Use three strands of embroidery thread at all times. Starting at the end of the strip work the narrow border design centrally along the fabric until your embroidery is slightly longer than the width of the towel. Once your border strip is complete remove the fabric from the frame. Press on the wrong side, if necessary, with a steam iron.

3 Carefully trim away the excess fabric leaving four sets of Aida threads along each long side of the embroidery.

Trim the excess fabric from the ends of the strip, leave a small turning allowance at each end.

4 Place the trimmed strip across one end of your guest towel so that it covers the woven band. Pin and tack (baste) it into position, tucking in the raw ends between the border and the towel.

5 With white sewing thread on the top of your sewing machine and blue in the spool (bobbin), work a line of wide satin stitch along both edges of the border, covering them with the width of the stitching. This will neatly and securely attach the strip to the towel. Alternatively this may be hand sewn (see Basic Stitches and Techniques, page 15).

NOTE: If you have used the scalloped edge Aida band you can attach it to your towel by machine straight stitches or hand back stitches.

6 To finish, neatly slip stitch the tucked in ends of the bands to the sides of the towel.

TO MAKE THE HAND TOWEL BORDER

Work this in the same way as the Guest Towel, using the wider strip or band of fabric and embroidering the wider border design.

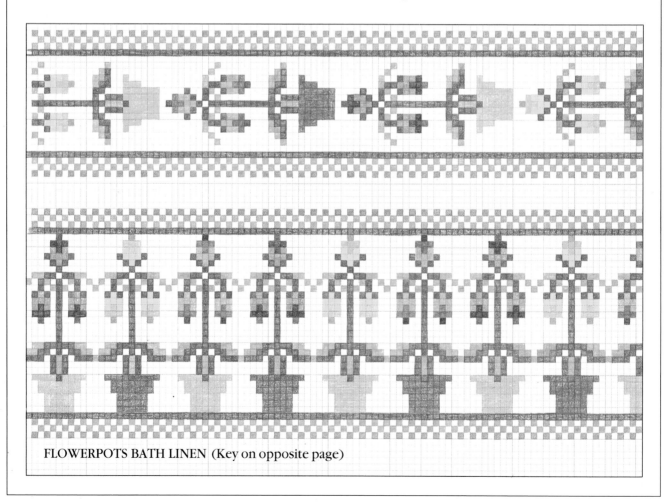

FLOWERPOTS BATH LINEN (Key on opposite page)

WASHING LINE BED LINEN

THE LOVELY CUSHION DESIGN on page 55 has been adapted for use on this bed linen. The design could also be used on towels or picnic linen. I have used the lines of washing, repeating them across a single duvet cover. The pretty motif on the pillowcase is the central section on the cover design. If you find the length of the duvet border a daunting prospect, work a smaller strip to decorate a pillowcase.

MATERIALS

White Aida fabric (Zweigart E3706) 14-count, one piece 8in (20cm) square, and one piece 8 x 56in (20 x 142cm)

DMC stranded cotton (floss): 2 skeins each Green 3816, 3348; Rust 356; 1 skein each blue 800, 3807; Mauve 552, 3608; Pink 963; Yellow 745; Orange 742; Flesh 945

White sewing thread

Blue-and-white striped cotton single duvet cover and matching pillowcase

Wooden embroidery hoop, 6in (15cm) diameter

Small rotating frame

NOTE: You may choose to use the same scalloped edge Aida band as suggested on page 57 for the towels. If you do then use the 4in (10cm) width band.

TO MAKE THE PILLOWCASE MOTIF

1 Place the square of Aida fabric in your hoop and pull it gently to ensure the grain is straight. Use three strands of thread at all times. Find the centre stitch of the stretched fabric by counting the sets of threads and follow the cushion chart shown on page 56 and work the small centre square. Ensure all your cross stitches are constructed in the same way to give a neat and even effect.

2 When your design is complete remove the fabric from the hoop and press it on the wrong side using a steam iron.

3 Trim away the excess fabric leaving four sets of Aida threads on all sides of the embroidered square.

4 Place the motif on the pillowcase near to a corner, at the open end of the case. You will see I have chosen to position my motif so that it appears as a diamond. When you are satisfied with the position carefully tack (baste) it in place. Take care not to tack (baste) it through all the layers of the pillowcase. Then, with white sewing thread, machine a wide line of satin stitch along the raw edge of the Aida fabric to neatly and securely attach the motif in position. Once more take care not to stitch through the layers of the pillowcase.

5 Press carefully on the wrong side with a steam iron.

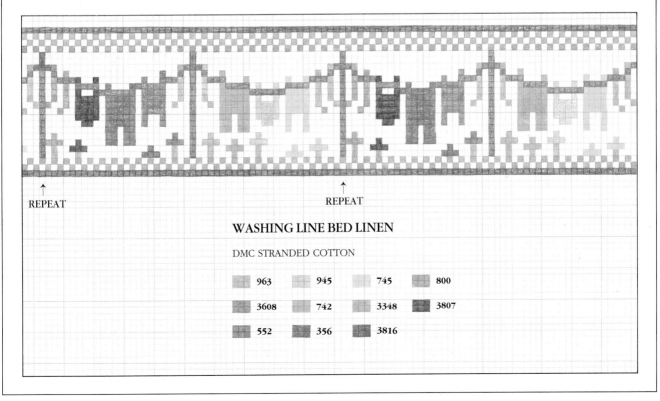

↑
REPEAT

↑
REPEAT

WASHING LINE BED LINEN

DMC STRANDED COTTON

	963		945		745		800
	3608		742		3348		3807
	552		356		3816		

TO MAKE THE DUVET BORDER

This may be worked freely in the hand, in the hoop or on the rotating frame. I chose to use the rotating frame as the surplus fabric is kept rolled up neatly. If using a hoop you will have to repeatedly re-position the fabric, so there is a greater risk of it becoming soiled and crumpled.

1 Mount the fabric in the frame or hoop. Beginning close to one end of the Aida strip, centre the design across the width of the fabric and commence stitching. Follow the repeat chart on page 59. I found it a great help to start by working the brown washing line and then use this as a guide to work the rest of the design around. Repeat the design over and over again until you have worked slightly more than the width of the duvet cover.

2 Remove the fabric from the frame. If necessary press it gently on the wrong side, using a steam iron.

3 Trim away the excess fabric along the sides of the strip. Reserve these side pieces to use later to make gift cards (see page 62). Leave four sets of Aida threads on each side of the embroidered strip. Lay the strip across one end of the duvet cover to compare the width of the duvet and the length of the strip. Leave a small turning allowance at each end of the strip and cut off the excess.

4 Pin the border strip in position across the duvet cover approximately 13in (33cm) from the top edge.

5 Carefully unpick 4in (10cm) of the seam at each side of the duvet where the border strip will lie. Tuck in the strip and tack (baste) it into position.

6 With white sewing thread machine stitch a wide line of satin stitch along the raw edge of each side of the strip to neatly and securely attach it.

7 Working from the inside of the duvet cover, pin the unpicked seams together and re-stitch. Press the duvet carefully with a steam iron to finish.

FLOWERPOT &
BASKET PICTURES

USING THE SAME FABRIC and threads as the cushion, towels and bed linen, I have designed a set of four small pictures (see page 64). I have mounted them in plain green frames to show off their freshness and simplicity. They are very pretty but so quick and easy to make and can be mounted as greetings cards if you prefer.

MATERIALS

White Aida fabric (Zweigart E3706), 14-count, 4 pieces
  each 10in (25cm) square
DMC stranded cotton (floss): 1 skein each Green 3348,
  3816; Rust 356; Blue 800, 3807; Mauve 552, 3608; Pink 963;
  Orange 742; Flesh 945
Strong buttonhole thread, any colour
4 pieces firm, white mounting cardboard, each measuring
  5 x 7in (12.5 x 17.5cm) or to fit chosen frame
4 wooden frames with mounts of suitable size
Wooden embroidery hoop, 7in (18cm) diameter
NOTE: You may find it advisable to work the four small designs before purchasing your frames and mounts as you may wish to choose something quite different to those shown on page 64. The frames I have used have a window measurement of 5½ x 7½in (14 x 19cm) and the window mounts have an inside measurement of 4 x 6in (10 x 15cm).

TO MAKE THE PICTURES

1 Work one motif at a time. Mount the fabric within your hoop, gently pulling the fabric so that the grain is straight and the fabric taut.

2 Use three strands of thread at all times. Follow each chart, positioning the motif centrally on your fabric. You will see that the butterflies have tiny antennae. These are worked in a single straight stitch or a few back stitches (see Basic Stitches and Techniques, page 13).

3 When the stitchery is complete remove the fabric from the hoop and press it gently on the wrong side with a steam iron.

4 Place the fabric over the mounting card so that the embroidery is centred. Trim away the excess fabric leaving at least 1¼in (3cm) turning allowance on each side. Use strong buttonhole thread to lace the fabric in position over the cardboard. (See Basic Stitches and Techniques, page 15). Now place the stretched embroidery in the chosen frame and mount. Repeat steps 1–4 with each of the four designs.

A delightful small card or gift tag has been created simply by working one of the flowerpot motifs with a border around it. I used a small offcut of the Aida fabric from one of the other projects and then mounted the motif in a blank greetings card that I made to the correct size (see Basic Stitches and Techniques page 15).

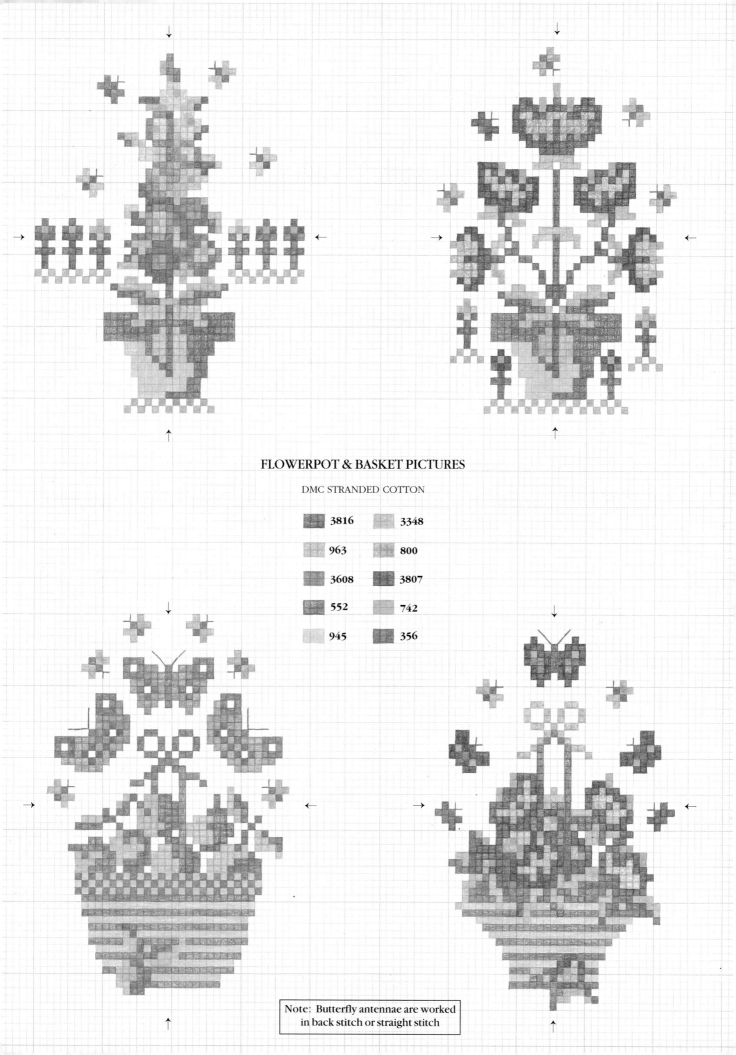

FLOWERPOT & BASKET PICTURES

DMC STRANDED COTTON

3816		3348	
963		800	
3608		3807	
552		742	
945		356	

Note: Butterfly antennae are worked
in back stitch or straight stitch

CHAPTER 5

The Autumn Garden

TO ME, IMAGES OF autumn include galloping as a child through wind-tossed piles of brittle brown leaves searching excitedly for conkers and other seasonal treasures; fingertips stained purple and prickling with pain from gathering juicy black fruits from brambles; flower beds once overflowing with colour becoming tousled and tired; heavily laden apple and pear trees dropping their rich harvest of fruits onto dew-soaked grass.

With so many inspiring thoughts in my mind I chose an all-time favourite theme of blackberries and apples, as together their distinctive shape and colouring provide wonderful scope for attractive designs.

At the far end of my garden I am very lucky to have an extensive bramble thicket that is quite impenetrable but bears wonderfully juicy blackberries – for the birds as well as my family. I also have several very old and gnarled apple trees which produce lots of sweet and colourful fruit. These two plants yielded plenty of inspiration and reference material to create the following luscious designs.

BLACKBERRY & APPLE CUSHION

Having gathered an armful of barbed bramble stems I began to make several drawings and design sketches. I was intrigued by the variety of colours and the beauty of this rather spiteful plant. Serrated-edged leaves point boldly while berries hang in tiny clusters of sparkling jewels. The russet-red and green colouring of the small round apples acts as a contrast and lightens the design.

MATERIALS

Cream 264 Aida fabric (Zweigart E3706), 14-count, 20in (50cm) square

Cream fabric suitable for the cushion back, 16in (40cm) square (I used a lightweight furnishing brocade)

Cream or white cotton backing fabric, two pieces each 16in (40cm) square

DMC stranded cotton (floss): 3 skeins Green 991; 2 skeins each Green 987, 3816; Plum 3802; 1 skein each Green 906, 3348, 3819; Mauve 327; Magenta 915; Red 304; Smoky Pink 3722; Orange 900, 977; Brown 611

Green cord to compliment bramble leaves, 1¾yd (1.6m) (I used a cord curtain tieback)

Green sewing thread to match cord

Cream sewing thread

Cushion pad, 15in (38cm) square

Wooden embroidery frame, 17in (43cm) square

TO MAKE THE CUSHION

1 To work the embroidery, mount the cream Aida fabric onto your frame ensuring the fabric grain is parallel to the sides of the frame.

2 Find and mark with tacking (basting) stitches the centre hole of the fabric.

3 Work the embroidery using three strands of thread at all times and ensure all your cross stitches are constructed in the same way to give a neat and even effect. Also check every now and then to make sure your stitching is accurate, as with this sort of very full and complicated design it is easy to jump a square without noticing, putting the whole design out of alignment.

Count outwards from the centre, along one of the tacked guidelines, to where the point of a bramble leaf coincides with the guideline. Start by stitching the plum-coloured veins of this and the adjoining leaves to give you a framework on which to build, then build up the design gradually.

4 Once you have completed the stitchery remove the fabric from the frame.

5 To make the cushion accurately count twenty-seven sets of threads or squares from the outermost leaf tips around each side of the design to establish the seam line. Mark with a pin on each side. Count a further six sets of threads and accurately cut along this line on each side to trim away the excess fabric of the cushion front.

6 Place one of the cream backing squares under the wrong side of the embroidered fabric. Join the layers by accurately machine straight stitching in cream sewing thread along the marked seam line.

7 Place the remaining cream backing square under the wrong side of the ivory brocade fabric (to add support to the fabric). Then, with right sides together, place the embroidered fabric over the brocade so that the backing layers are outermost. Pin, tack (baste) and machine straight stitch accurately along the seam line, starting at one corner and finishing halfway along the fourth side to leave an opening.

8 Trim the layers of fabric across the corners of the seam allowance and turn the cushion carefully to the right side. If necessary press the cover gently on the wrong side with an iron to remove any creases that may have occurred.

9 Place the cushion pad inside the cover. Fold in the edges of the opening and pin to hold in position. Slip stitch along the opening leaving a small gap at the corner. Do not finish off the thread at this point.

10 Tuck one end of the green decorative cord into the tiny opening at this corner and with double thickness matching thread, slip stitch the cord around the cushion sides. When you arrive back at the starting point cut off the excess cord allowing a small amount to be pushed neatly into the seam gap. With a little patience you will find you can make the cord appear to be continuous. Close the seam line gap with cream thread and finish off neatly. NOTE: Some cords unravel quickly when cut. To prevent this happening bind the cut ends with thread or temporarily with adhesive tape.

BLACKBERRY AND APPLE CUSHION

DMC STRANDED COTTON

327	3722	991	987	3819	611	900
915	3802	3816	906	3348	304	977

HERB PILLOW

*FOR THIS CHARMING HERB pillow I have used the same rich colours as on the
Blackberry and Apple Cushion, stylising and greatly simplifying the bramble fruits
and leaves until they have become part of a delightfully simple geometric pattern.
Once more the rich colours of the little round apples add an extra quality and
warmth to this quickly and easily worked design.*

MATERIALS

Cream 264 Aida fabric (Zweigart E3706), 14-count, 11in
(28cm) square

Cream fabric suitable for the pillow back, 6in (15cm)
square (I used the same fabric as for the cushion)

Cream or white cotton backing fabric, two pieces each 6in
(15cm) square

DMC stranded cotton (floss): 1 skein each Green 906, 987,
991, 3348, 3816, 3819; Plum 3802; Mauve 327; Magenta
915; Red 304; Smoky Pink 3722; Orange 900, 977;
Brown 611

Cream gathered-cotton lace edging, ¾in (2cm) wide x 24in
(60cm) long

Cream sewing thread

Small amount of Terylene or polyester filling
Small amount of pot-pourri
Wooden embroidery hoop, 8in (20cm) diameter

TO MAKE THE PILLOW

1 Place the cream Aida fabric centrally within the hoop
ensuring the grain of the fabric is straight. Find and mark
with tacking (basting) stitches the centre hole of the fabric.

2 Work the embroidery using three strands of thread at
all times. You will find it beneficial to work outwards
from the central motif, completing your design with the
outer border.

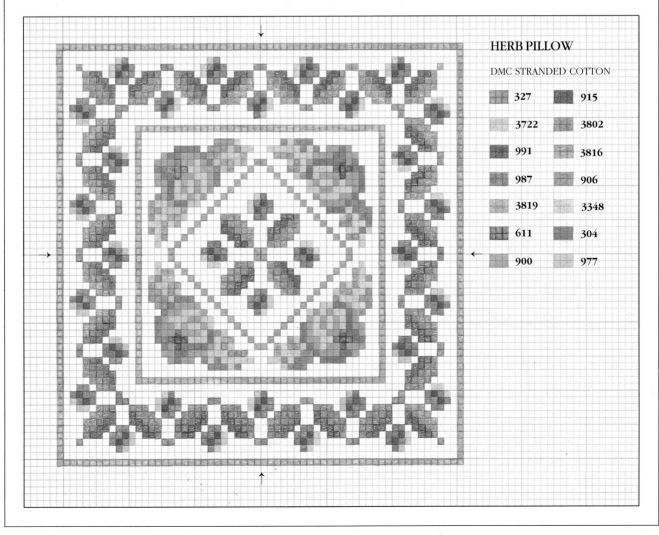

HERB PILLOW

DMC STRANDED COTTON

	327		915
	3722		3802
	991		3816
	987		906
	3819		3348
	611		304
	900		977

3 Remove the fabric from the hoop and carefully press it on the wrong side with a steam iron. Count ten sets of threads outwards from the edge of the green border line of stitches and cut along this line on each side to trim away the excess fabric.

4 Place one of the cream backing squares under the Aida fabric and machine straight stitch around your design on the seam line (which is four sets of threads away from the green border), then pin the gathered lace edging along this line.

5 Place the remaining backing square under the ivory brocade square and pin together. With right sides facing

pin and tack (baste) these layers to the prepared Aida square, ensuring that the fullness of the gathered lace edging is not caught in the seam line at the corners. Machine straight stitch along the seam line, remembering to leave an opening of approximately 2¼in (5.5cm) along one side.

6 Trim the seam allowance across corners. Turn the Herb Pillow to the right side and gently ease into shape. Press gently on the wrong side with a steam iron if necessary.

7 Place your chosen filling inside the pillow and add some pot-pourri. Turn in the raw edges of the opening and close with tiny slip stitches.

AUTUMN GIFT TAGS

THESE PRETTY LITTLE TAGS have been created by simply working the centre motif of the Herb Pillow. After stitching the motif I selected a gift card and worked two lines of green border stitches around the motif to fit the card (see picture, page 72). It is often much easier to work your embroidery to fit the card rather than get a card to fit your embroidery.

MATERIALS
Cream 264 Aida fabric (Zweigart E3706), 14-count, minimum size 3in (7.5cm) square
DMC stranded cotton (floss): small amounts of Green 987, 991, 3816; Mauve 327; Plum 3802; Magenta 915; Smoky Pink 3722
Cream gift tags or cards (DMC Chelsea Studio Cards, N2399 Cream)
Clear adhesive suitable for paper and fabric

TO MAKE THE GIFT TAGS

1 Using three strands of thread at all times, hand hold the small piece of Aida fabric to work the delightfully simple blackberry design.

NOTE: You will need to take extra care when holding the fabric in your hand rather than in a frame in order to achieve a neat and even tension with your stitching.
  If you want to make several gift tags at the same time I recommend working the motifs together using a larger piece of fabric stretched in a hoop or frame.

2 When you have completed the motif press the fabric gently on the wrong side using a steam iron. Trim away three sets of threads on each side of your embroidery.

3 Using the glue sparingly, carefully position the fabric within the window of your gift tag. Complete the tag by gluing the backing section in position behind the wrong side of the motif.

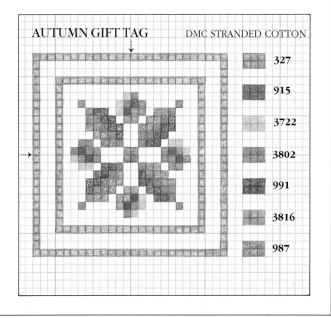

AUTUMN GIFT TAG — DMC STRANDED COTTON

	327
	915
	3722
	3802
	991
	3816
	987

Opposite: The glowing autumnal colours of bottled preserves made by my grandmother linger in my mind and have inspired these charmingly simple designs

FOOTSTOOL

WHAT COULD BE BETTER *than to sit with one's feet on such a welcoming stool as this, while outside the autumn gales strip the leaves from the trees? I have chosen a beautifully crafted hexagonal teak stool which compliments and echoes the stylised shape of the bramble berries. You could however use any shape of stool as the embroidered design is an all-over repeat pattern allowing you to work the embroidery to fit whatever shape or size required. I found this project surprisingly quick to complete as each cross stitch is worked over two horizontal and two vertical threads of canvas producing a closely stitched area of embroidery. You could experiment with working on a different scale by choosing a finer yarn and canvas or evenweave fabric.*

MATERIALS

White single-thread canvas (Zweigart E1281), 14-count, 20in (50cm) square

DMC tapestry wool: 5 skeins Green 7428; 4 skeins each Green 7342, 7384; 3 skeins each Green 7542; Light Stone 7500; Red 7107; 2 skeins each Purple 7257, 7266; Green 7361,7584; Orange 7439; 1 skein each Magenta 7157; Smoky Pink 7195; Orange 7918; Brown 7415

Hexagonal teak footstool (Woodhouse DF121) 13in (33cm) from side to side (see Suppliers, page 127)

Wooden frame 18in (46cm) square

Upholstery tacks (or staples)

TO MAKE THE FOOTSTOOL

1 Stretch the canvas on the frame, ensuring the threads are parallel to the sides of the frame.

2 Carefully make a paper pattern of the shape and size of the raised padded area of the footstool. Add an extra ⅜in (1cm) all around for a turning allowance. Cut out the paper pattern. Pin it centrally onto the stretched canvas and tack (baste) around the edges to give you the minimum area which has to be embroidered. Remove the paper pattern.

NOTE: Use your woollen yarn as economically as possible and always begin and finish off the yarn ends neatly and securely. Never jump across the wrong side of the canvas from one area to another, but finish off and start again. Avoid using very long lengths of yarn. Passing it backwards and forwards through the holes of the tough canvas will gradually wear it thin. Do not be tempted to try to scoop the needle down and up through the canvas

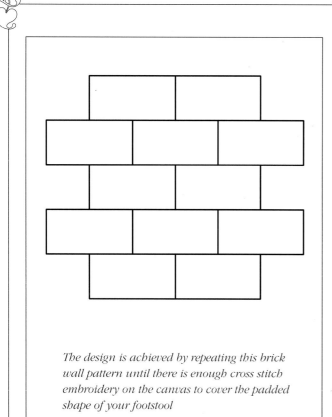

The design is achieved by repeating this brick wall pattern until there is enough cross stitch embroidery on the canvas to cover the padded shape of your footstool

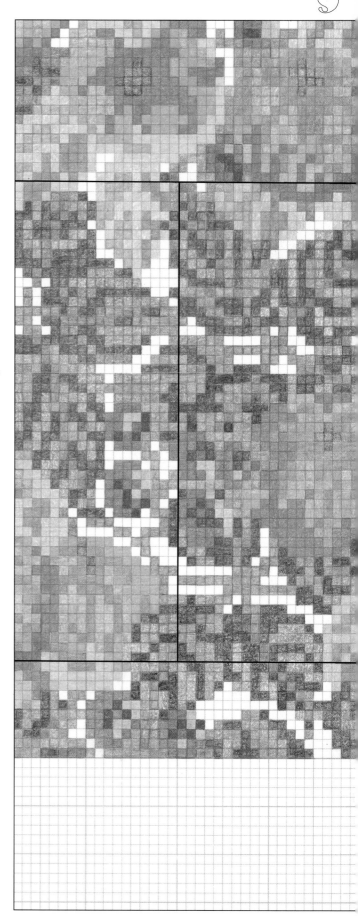

in one movement as this will strain the canvas and give a distorted uneven end result. Working on a frame should prevent you doing this and help avoid having to damp stretch your finished work.

3 As this design is an all-over pattern it does not really matter where you start as there is no beginning and end to it. I chose to place the star-like motif of the bramble leaves in the top right of the design in the middle of the canvas, working the plum-coloured leaf veins to give a good starting point around which to build. All the tiny light stone background shapes can be worked last of all.

4 When the stitchery is complete remove the canvas from the frame. Check that the stitched area will cover the raised pad of the stool before trimming away the excess canvas. (You may need to add a few extra stitches around the edges.) Leave enough canvas to enable you to stretch it over and around the pad. Fix in position using upholstery tacks or staples and a staple gun.

5 Place the covered pad into the wooden stool frame and screw securely in position.

The chart shows one complete 'brick' from the repeat pattern that makes up the all-over design for the footstool

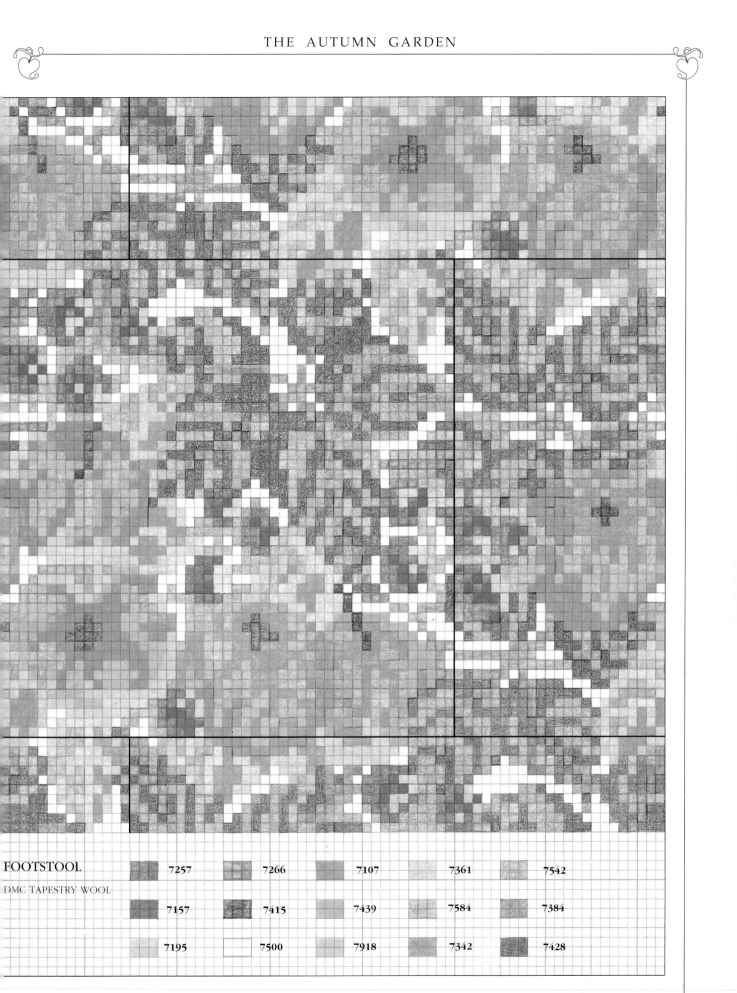

FOOTSTOOL

DMC TAPESTRY WOOL

7257	7266	7107	7361	7542
7157	7415	7439	7584	7384
7195	7500	7918	7342	7428

HARVEST OF IDEAS

THE FOLLOWING PROJECTS GIVE you some idea of the versatility of the designs in this book. For the first two projects I have extracted parts of the Herb Pillow chart to work some beautiful gift items. In the third project, Autumn Circlets, I have provided two additional charts designed to use up spare bits of thread.

BRAMBLE PINCUSHION

For this pretty pincushion I have extracted my bramble motif from the Herb Pillow and adapted it to produce an all-over repeat pattern. This could be used for many ideas. For example, if you enlarge the scale or working and use tapestry wools on canvas you could produce a quick-growing design for a cushion or footstool.

I have chosen to work only a small piece using the same fabrics and threads as before and have mounted the fabric in a beautifully made teak pincushion (Double pincushion, DF102, Woodhouse – see Suppliers, page 127). The padded and embroidered lid lifts off to reveal a useful pin or needle tray in the base.

BRAMBLE BATH LINEN

Once more I have made use of the bramble design from the Herb Pillow. I have simply worked the outer border design to fit the width of a cream hand towel and matching face-cloth. I chose the same fabric and threads as in the earlier projects, trimming away the excess fabric and attaching the border strip to the towelling by neat and secure lines of wide machine satin stitch. You could just as effectively use one of the many Aida bands, for example Zweigart E7107, cream 2in (5cm) wide.

AUTUMN CIRCLETS

These dainty circlets have a dual purpose – not only do they look beautiful as table mats but they can also be used as jar or jug covers. Simply choose an elegant jar with a fairly small opening. Fill this with pot-pourri or herbs, cover with the embroidered circlet and hold it in place with a satin ribbon. The perfume from the contents will slowly be released through the fabric. For a jug cover sew some pretty beads around the lace edging to hang down and hold the cover in position over a cream or milk jug.

The fabric used here is cream 264 Linda 27-count fabric (Zweigart E1235), if you wish to make the circlets as jam pot covers to fit a standard pot with a 2½in (6cm) opening, use a larger gauge fabric (Aida 11-count, Zweigart E1007). This will produce a bolder design that will lay around the edge of the fabric below the rim of the jam pot when held in place with a ribbon. Instructions for making similar circlets can be found on page 106.

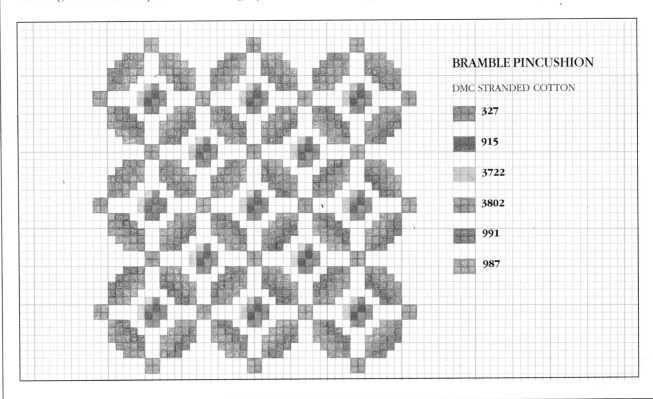

BRAMBLE PINCUSHION

DMC STRANDED COTTON

- 327
- 915
- 3722
- 3802
- 991
- 987

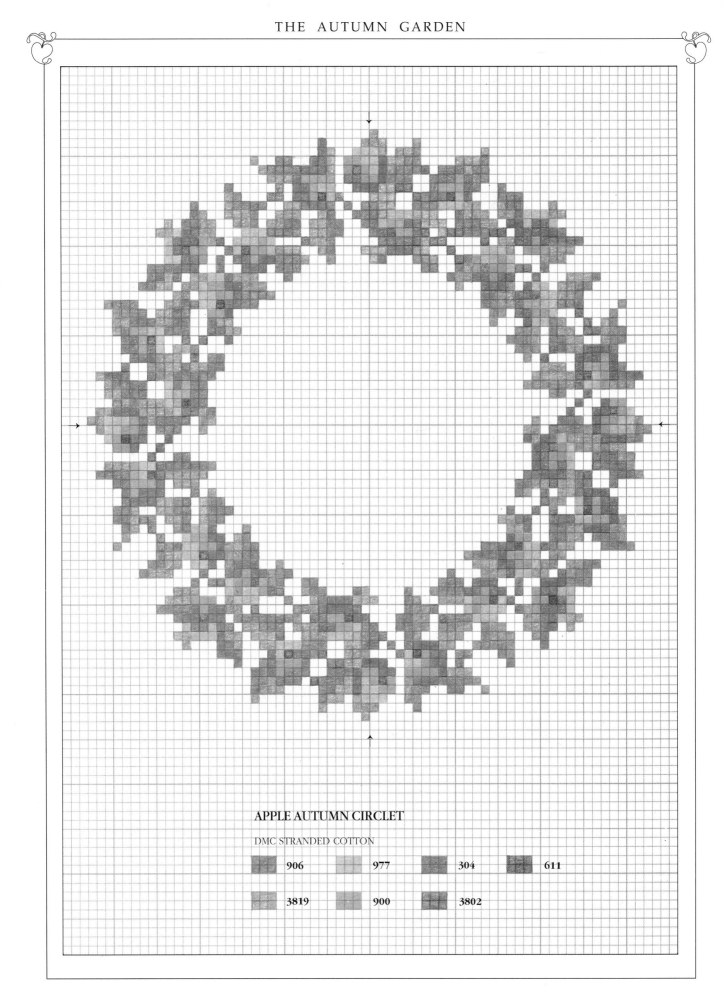

APPLE AUTUMN CIRCLET

DMC STRANDED COTTON

	906		977		304		611
	3819		900		3802		

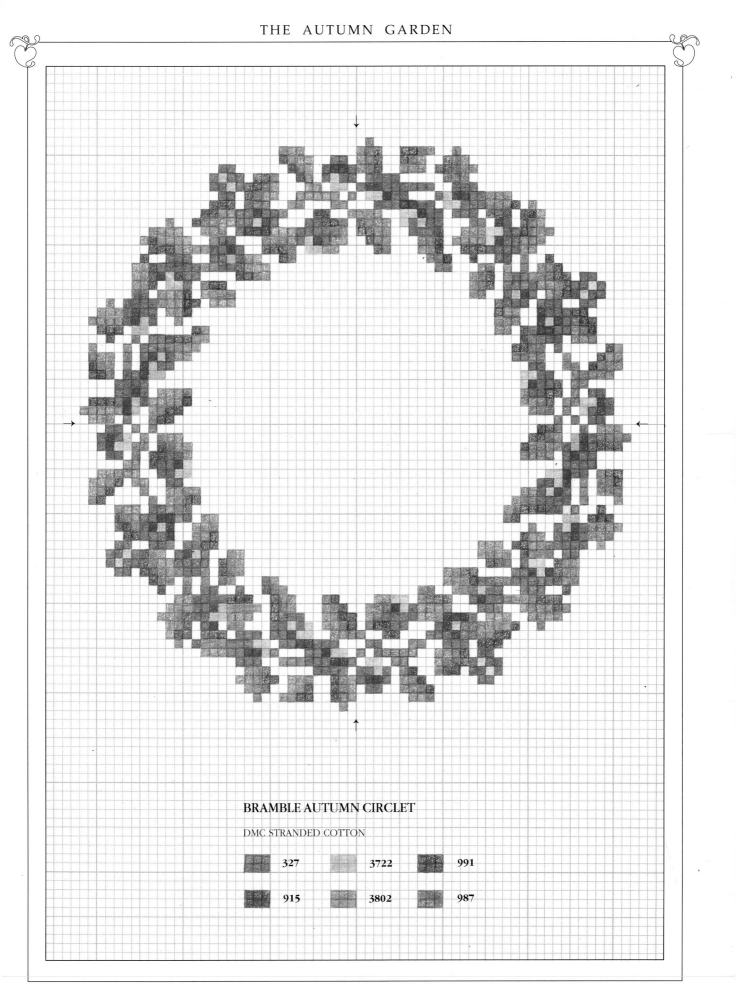

BRAMBLE AUTUMN CIRCLET

DMC STRANDED COTTON

327	3722	991
915	3802	987

CHAPTER 6

Yesterday's Garden

THE SIGHT OF KNOT gardens, parterres and topiary will always evoke wonderfully romantic images. Mix this with sundials and dovecots, beehives and clipped conifers in stone pots and you have scenes from yesteryear that can easily be adapted and translated into stitchery. In this chapter I have done just this and the result is a nostalgic selection characterised by fresh colouring and simple motifs with a hint of formality in the designs.

As with the other chapters there is a wealth of design material for you to enjoy using and all the projects reflect quiet past elegance and subtlety. You might start by making the beautiful herb pillow, with its subtle scent, intricate stitchery and fascinating design. The four framed wall pictures are highly decorative and would be ideal for your home or as individual gifts. The pincushion and needle case would also make lovely gifts – not only are they charming and easy to make but very useful. Or you could start with something ultra-simple, like the tiny gift cards featuring four charming motifs.

HERB CUSHION

THE DELIGHTFUL AROMA FROM this cushion, which features a central cross-stitch panel with a simple geometric pattern and tiny garden motifs, is reminiscent of knot gardens filled with herbs. The design could also be mounted, framed and hung as a wall picture. The background fabric should compliment the design, so work the embroidery and then select a fabric with a small, simple pattern.

MATERIALS

Cream 264, Aida fabric (Zweigart E3706), 14-count, 13½in (34cm) square

DMC stranded cotton (floss): 2 skeins each Green 3347, 3814; 1 skein each Yellow 743; Pink 917, 3609; Lavender 3746, 3747; Grey 414; Beige 842

DMC coton perlé No 5 thread: 1 skein Green 3347

Cotton lawn printed fabric, 28in (70cm) of 45in (115cm) wide

Cream cotton backing fabric, two pieces each 13in (33cm) square

Sewing thread, cream and sage-green to match coton perlé thread

Cushion pad with polyester or Terylene filling, 12in (30cm) square

Small amount of pot-pourri (lavender or other herbal mix)

Cotton fabric, 10in (25cm) square (to make a sachet to hold pot-pourri)

Cream cotton lace edging, 1⅝yd (1.5m), ⅝in (1.5cm) wide

Wooden embroidery frame, 12in (30cm) square

TO MAKE THE CUSHION

1 To work the embroidery, mount the Aida fabric onto your embroidery frame ensuring the grain of the material is parallel to the sides of the frame.

2 Find and mark, with tacking (basting) stitches, the centre hole of the fabric.

3 Work the embroidery using three strands of cotton (floss) at all times. You will find it beneficial to start by working the centre square and then gradually build up the outlines of the surrounding squares and cross shapes before working all the little stylised plants and garden motifs.

Ensure all the cross stitches are constructed in the same way to give a neat and even effect. This is particularly important with the outer sage-green areas as any uneven stitchery will show up.

4 Once you have completed the stitchery then remove the fabric from the frame. Trim away the excess fabric leaving three sets of threads around each side of the embroidery. Reserve the surplus strips to make tiny gift tags or bookmarks.

5 Use a ⅜in (1cm) seam allowance unless otherwise directed. Lay the cotton print fabric upon a clean, flat surface making sure it is crease-free. Carefully measure and then cut two 6in (15cm) wide strips across the width of the fabric (from selvedge to selvedge). Reserve these for the cushion frill.

6 From the remaining cotton print fabric measure and carefully cut out two 13in (33cm) squares. Position these to one side of the fabric so that you are as economical as possible with it. Reserve the left-over piece as it can be used with the pincushion and needle case projects (see page 88).

7 With right sides uppermost, place one print square on top of a cream backing square, aligning their edges. Then on top of these centrally place your trimmed embroidered square, positioning it so that the corners of the embroidered fabric are at the mid-points of the sides of the print fabric. Use a ruler or tape measure to help you. Tack (baste) the layers of fabric together. With cream thread machine satin stitch along the cut edge of the Aida fabric to securely and neatly join the fabrics.

8 To make the frill start by joining, with right sides together, the two long strips of print fabric to form a continuous band. With right sides outwards fold the band in half along its length to give a double layer 3in (7.5cm) wide. Press with an iron to give a crisp folded edge. Along the raw double edge work two lines of gathering stitches, either by hand or by machine. Work these lines just on the outside of the seam allowance. With right sides together pin and tack (baste) the gathered frill around the cushion face, arranging the gathers evenly and ensuring there are ample gathers at the corners. Machine straight stitch along the seam line to attach the frill to the cushion face. Clip across the corners of the seam allowance to remove the excess fabric.

9 With right side uppermost place the remaining print fabric square on top of the backing square, aligning their edges. Place the cushion front (face downwards) on top of these layers. Pin and tack (baste) together ensuring the frills are folded away from the seam line. Machine straight stitch along the seam line taking care not to catch the folds of the frill in the stitching. Leave an opening of 8in

(20cm) along one side. Trim the seam allowance at the corners, then gently turn the cushion to the right side, trying not to crease the fabric.

10 To make the pot-pourri sachet fold the square of cotton fabric in half and machine straight stitch around two of the sides leaving the third open. Turn to the right side and fill with pot-pourri. If your pot-pourri contains large, hard pieces (seeds or seed pods) then omit these, using only the smaller or crushed petals and leaves. Fold in and pin together the open edges of the sachet; then machine straight stitch along them to close.

11 Carefully unpick a little of the stitching on one side of the cushion pad. Push the pot-pourri sachet into the centre of the filling inside the cushion, then re-stitch the open seam line to close.

12 Insert cushion pad inside the cushion cover. Fold in raw edges of the opening and close with tiny slip stitches.

13 Apply the lace edging by hand with cream sewing thread. Beginning at one corner slip stitch the straight edge of the lace to the seam line of the cushion. At each corner take tiny tucks in the lace so that there is some fullness to allow you to follow around the shape of the cushion. When you have stitched the edging all the way round the cushion make the lace edging at the fourth corner match the others in its fullness before you cut off the excess edging. Carefully stitch the raw ends of the lace together to neaten.

14 Finally, make a twisted cord. Carefully and patiently unravel the skein of green coton perlé thread and divide

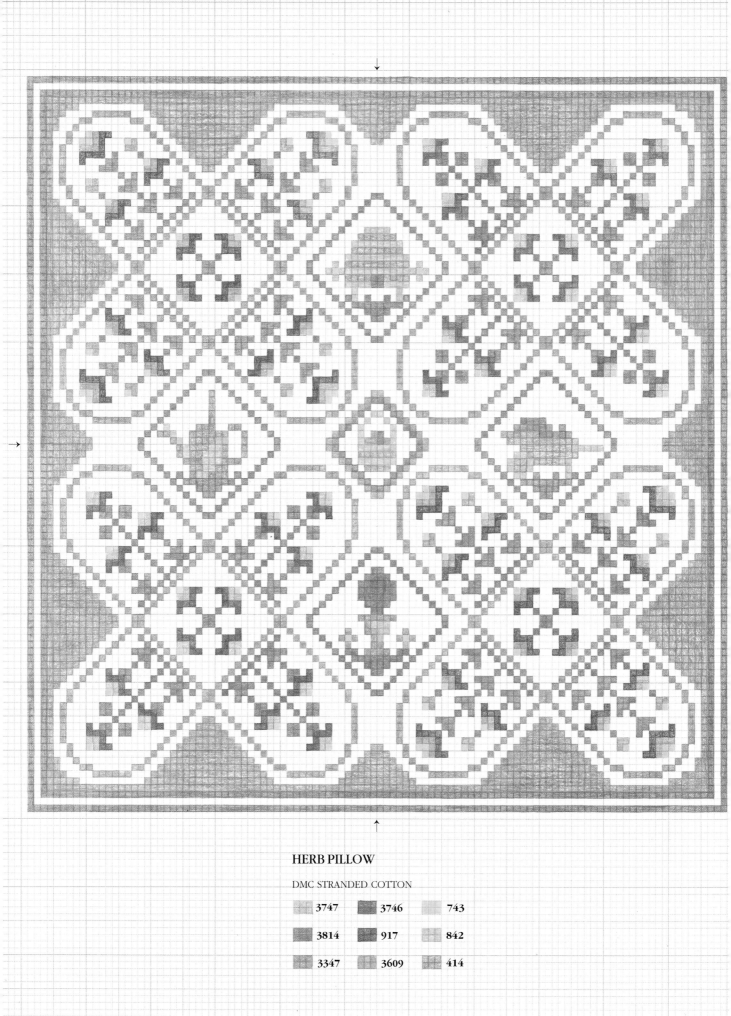

HERB PILLOW

DMC STRANDED COTTON

3747		3746		743	
3814		917		842	
3347		3609		414	

it into four equal lengths. Tie the threads together at each end and use to make the cord (see Basic Stitches and Techniques page 14).

15 Stitch cord around the cushion starting and finishing at bottom corner of the cushion (so that tiny garden motifs are right way up). As you start to stitch cord around the cushion leave a loose hanging tail (with knotted end) 2½in (6cm) at bottom corner. Similarly leave the same amount hanging when you arrive back at this point. Neaten cord ends with mock tassels by teasing out cut thread ends. Arrange the hanging cords to look like a small bow then stitch into position.

GIFT CARDS OR TAGS

The tiny garden motifs within the inner squares of the knot garden design are just perfect for gift cards and tags (see photograph below). You can use some of the left-over strips of Aida from the Herb Cushion project, as the finished embroidery is only 2in (5cm) square. I have chosen dark green presentation cards (DMC Chelsea Studio Cards, N2399 Christmas Green) to mount the four designs within, adding an extra border of cross stitches in Green 3347 around the design and then working four tiny flowers around each of the motifs. The threads used were all surplus to the Herb Cushion project.

PINCUSHION & NEEDLE CASE

WITH MY MIND STILL buzzing with ideas of knot gardens and parterres I have designed two small squares which could easily be aerial views of box hedges clipped into intricate geometric patterns, separated by gravel paths and flower beds filled with flowers such as lavender and gilly flower. I have made these into a pincushion and needle case set, though you could make scented sachets, gift cards or other items.

MATERIALS

Cream 264 Aida fabric (Zweigart E3706), 14-count, 2 pieces each 8in (20cm) square

DMC stranded cotton (floss): 2 skeins Green 3347; 1 skein each Green 3814; Yellow 743; Pink 917, 3609; Lavender 3746, 3747

DMC coton perlé No 5 thread, 1 skein Green 3347 (or twisted cord left over from Herb Cushion project)

Cotton lawn printed fabric, four pieces each measuring 4¾in (12cm) square, taken from reserved fabric from Herb Cushion project

Cream cotton backing fabric, three pieces each 4¾in (12cm) square

Cream fine woollen fabric or felt, three pieces each 3½in (9cm) square

Heavyweight or pelmet interfacing (Vilene), two pieces each 3¾in (9.5cm) square

Small amount of Terylene or polyester filling

Sewing thread, cream and sage-green

Wooden embroidery hoop, 6in (15cm) diameter

Pinking shears

TO MAKE THE PINCUSHION

1 Mount one of the pieces of Aida fabric in the hoop ensuring the grain is straight. Find the centre hole of the fabric and mark with tacking (basting) stitches. Use three strands of embroidery thread at all times to work one of the two designs on pages 90 and 91. Start stitching in the centre of your chosen design, making sure all the cross stitches are constructed the same way to produce an even effect.

2 When your embroidery is complete remove the fabric from the hoop and press it gently on the wrong side using a steam iron to remove any creases and enhance the stitchery.

3 Trim away the excess fabric leaving four sets of threads around the outer line of stitching to become the seam allowance. With right side uppermost place the embroidered square centrally on top of one of the cream backing squares. Then with cream sewing thread carefully machine straight stitch around the embroidery, stitching along the line of holes next to the outer line of cross stitches. This is the seam guideline.

4 With right sides together place the cotton lawn print fabric and Aida squares together, then add the second square of cream backing fabric behind the print fabric. Pin and tack (baste) the layers together before machine straight stitching along the stitched guideline, remembering to leave a small opening for the filling. Clip across the seam allowance at the corners, then turn the pincushion to the right side.

5 Stuff the pincushion with your chosen filling. (I added a little pot-pourri as well to give a subtle aroma.) Fold in the open edges and with cream sewing thread slip stitch the edges together to close.

6 Use some of the twisted cord left over from the Herb Cushion project to stitch around the edges of the pincushion (see step 11, page 87). Leave a very short tail at each end of the cord and make into a mock tassel by teasing out the cut thread ends.

TO MAKE THE NEEDLE CASE

Follow steps 1–3 for making the pincushion.

4 With right sides together join carefully the Aida square with one of the cotton lawn print squares along one edge (on the stitched seam guideline). Similarly with right sides together join the other two print squares along one side. With right sides together place the joined Aida and print fabric piece on top of the double print piece, aligning the centre seam lines. Open these seams and finger press flat. Pin and tack (baste) around the edges. Machine straight stitch around the edges keeping accurately to the stitched guidelines of the Aida square and using these to measure, mark and stitch the second section, making it exactly the same size as the Aida section. Leave an opening of approximately 3in (7.5cm) centrally along one of the long sides.

5 Clip across the seam allowance at the corners then turn the needle case to the right side. With a steam iron carefully press the needle case into shape. Fold it in half along the centre seam line and press. Remember do not press directly onto the face of the Aida fabric as this will flatten your stitchery.

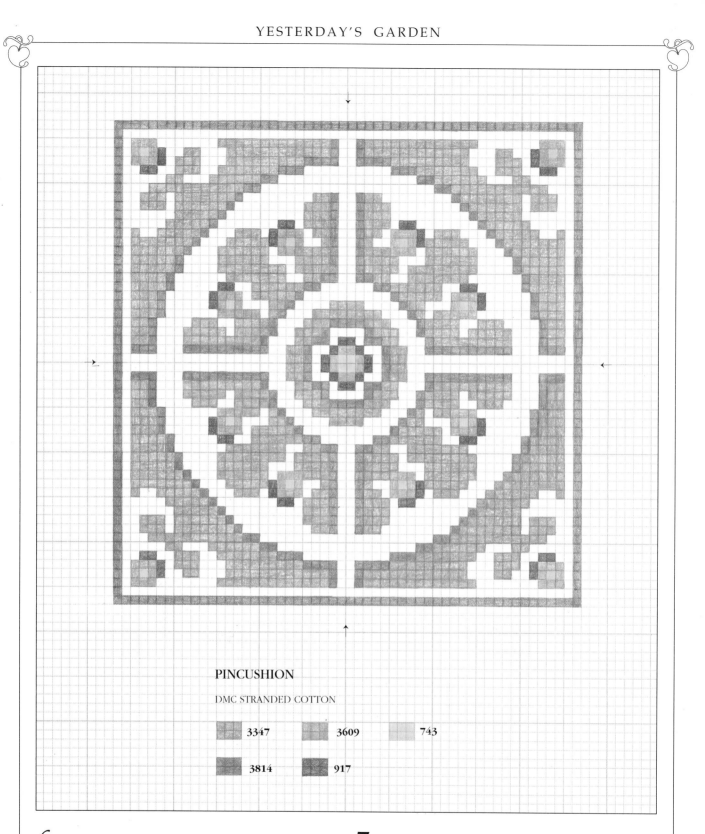

PINCUSHION

DMC STRANDED COTTON

▨	3347	▨	3609	▨	743
▨	3814	▨	917		

6 Trim the two squares of heavyweight interfacing so that each square is slightly smaller than the front and back of the needle case. Slip one of these squares in through the opening of the needle case, positioning it in front of the case. Similarly place the second square in the back of the case. Tuck in the edges of the opening and slip stitch the folded edges together to close. The interfacing will give a gentle firmness to the needle case.

7 Use remaining length of twisted cord left over from the Herb Cushion project. Start to attach the cord at the mid-point of the top (at the seam) of the folded needle case. With matching thread slip stitch the cord around the three sides of the back of the case. Continue along lower edge of the front, up and around the edges and finally down left edge of the front over the seam line. Neaten cord end with a knot and mock tassel by teasing out the thread ends.

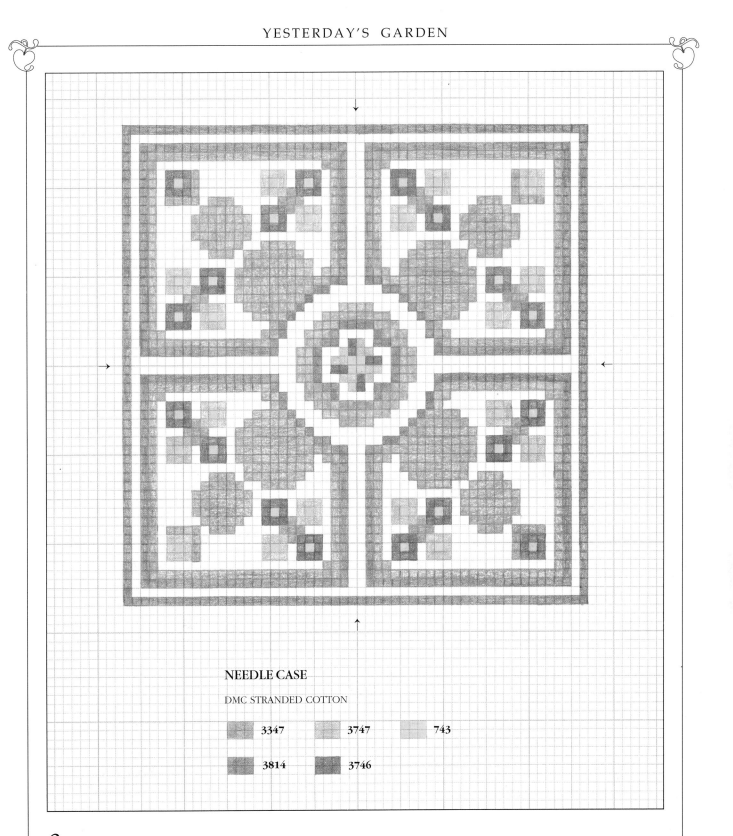

NEEDLE CASE

DMC STRANDED COTTON

3347	3747	743
3814	3746	

8 Finally, use pinking shears to trim the three cream woollen squares to measure 3⅛in (8cm) square. Open the needle case and place the woollen squares centrally on top of one another on the right-hand side of the open case. With cream sewing thread, machine straight stitch along the left-hand edge of the woollen squares attaching them securely to the needle case.

FOUR WALL PICTURES

*E*ACH OF THESE QUAINT *wall pictures has a simple, stylised garden object within
a pretty floral arch. The colours are the same as those used in the other projects
in this delightfully nostalgic chapter. I have chosen to mount and frame the motifs
(see page 94) but they could also be mounted within gift cards and given for
a special occasion perhaps for a wedding or on Valentine's Day.*

MATERIALS
Cream 264 Aida fabric (Zweigart E3706), 14-count, four
  pieces each 10in (25cm) square
DMC stranded cotton (floss): 1 skein each Green 3347,
  3814; Pink 917, 3609; Lavender 3746, 3747; Grey 414;
  Beige 842; Yellow 743
Firm white mounting cardboard – four pieces each 5 x 7in
  (12.5 x 17.5cm) or to fit chosen frames

Strong buttonhole thread, any colour
Wooden embroidery hoop, 8in (20cm) diameter
Four wooden frames with mounts of suitable size and
  colour
NOTE: You may find it advisable to work the designs
before purchasing your frames and mounts as you may
wish to choose something quite different to those shown.
The frames I have used have a window measurement of

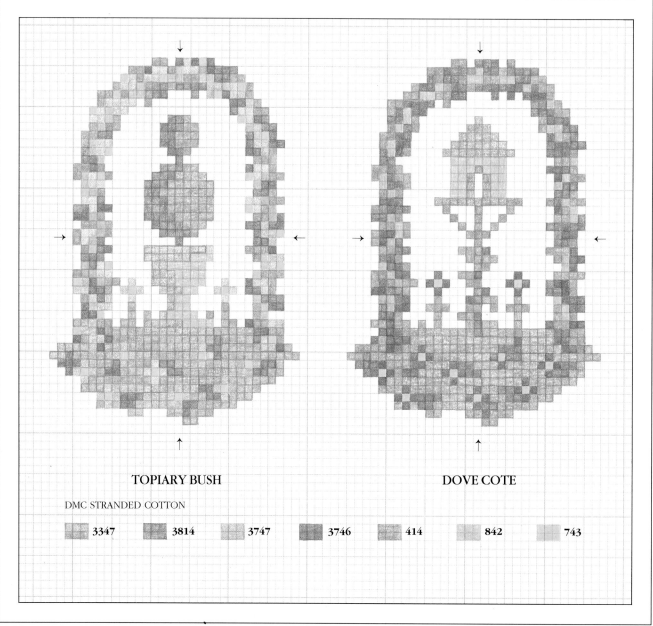

TOPIARY BUSH **DOVE COTE**

DMC STRANDED COTTON

| 3347 | 3814 | 3747 | 3746 | 414 | 842 | 743 |

5½ x 7½in (14 x 19cm) and the window mounts have an inside measurement of 4 x 6in (10 x 15cm) for the blue mount and 3¼ x 4¾in (8.5 x 12cm) for the smaller green mount.

TO WORK THE EMBROIDERY

1 Work one motif at a time. Mount the fabric within the hoop, gently pulling it so that the grain is straight and the fabric taut.

2 Use three strands of embroidery thread at all times and position each motif centrally upon the fabric. When working the sun dial motif use back stitches to add detail to the design (see Basic Stitches and Techniques page 13).

3 When the stitchery is complete remove from the hoop and press gently on the wrong side with a steam iron.

4 Place fabric over the mounting card so that the embroidery is centred. Trim away excess fabric leaving at least 1¼in (3cm) turning allowance on each side. Use strong buttonhole thread to lace the fabric centrally over the cardboard (see Basic Stitches and Techniques page 15). Now place the stretched embroidery in chosen frame and mount. Repeat steps 1–4 with each of the four designs.

NOTE: To mount the designs within blank gift cards DMC Chelsea Studio Cards N2390 in Stone, Pale Pink or Pale Blue would be ideal. Used in cards, the designs can also be worked on much smaller pieces of Aida fabric – 4 x 6in (10 x 15cm) – and embroidered in the hand.

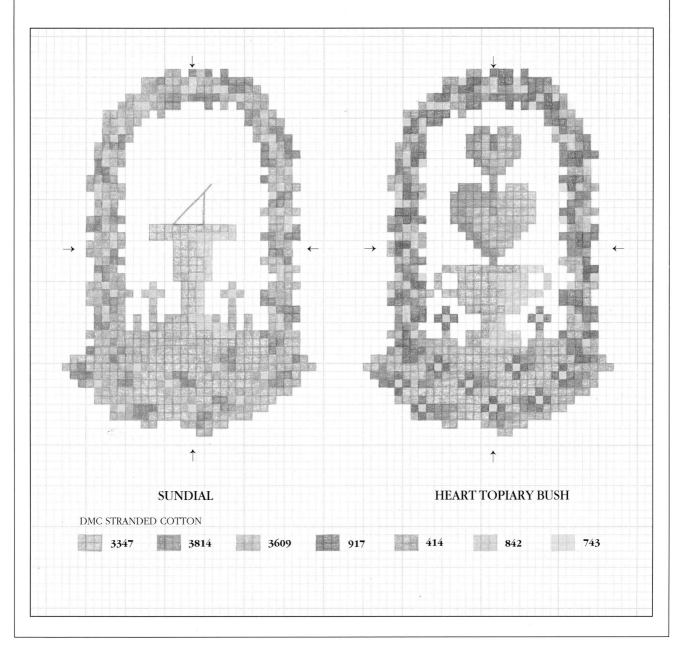

SUNDIAL   **HEART TOPIARY BUSH**

DMC STRANDED COTTON

	3347		3814		3609		917		414		842		743

CHAPTER 7

The Garden in Winter

DESPITE THE INCLEMENT WEATHER of winter there are still pockets of life to be found in the garden. Of course many of the colours are more subdued than those in summer and the vegetation is hardier, hugging close to the shelter of the ground. One of my favourite sights is the leathery green leaves that open out to reveal the cup-shaped nodding flowers of helleborus. With delicate hues from greenish-white through to smoky pinks and dusky purples, these flowers stand proudly confident on their sturdy stems, bringing beauty and hope to our gardens at a drab time of year.

So, with great enthusiasm I chose hellebores as the basis of my winter garden designs. Variegated ivy leaves – bright and cheerful with yellow centres, daintily pointed lobes and purplish berries – complement the helleborus flowers perfectly. Together they provided the inspiration for the lovely Hellebore and Ivy Cushion and from that design the other projects evolved. Part of the square border is used to edge bath linen and the Helleborus Hanging Sachet uses a cluster of helleborus and ivy in one striking motif. The main design has also been adapted to create jar covers, table mats, trinket boxes and gift cards.

HELLEBORE & IVY CUSHION

*WHEN WORKING ON A new design I find it so inspiring to have the subject matter
before me, to draw from real life, be aware of all the subtleties of colour, texture
and form so easily lost in a photograph. I gathered several wonderfully vigorous stems
of hellebores and some twining lengths of cheerful ivy and set about designing
this collection, producing first of all this gorgeous cushion.*

MATERIALS

White Aida fabric (Zweigart E3706), 14-count, 20in (50cm)
   square
Printed cotton fabric for back of cushion, 16in (40cm)
   square
White cotton backing fabric, two pieces each 16in (40cm)
   square
DMC stranded cotton (floss): 2 skeins each Green 501,
   989, 3363; Pink 543, 3727; Maroon 3803; Light Brown
   372; Mustard 734; 1 skein each Yellow 726, 745
White sewing thread
Cushion pad, 15in (38cm) square
Cord 1¾yd (1.6m) to compliment colours of design
   (I chose a cord curtain tieback with a soft mix of pinks
   and greens)
Sewing thread to match cord
Wooden frame, 17in (43cm) square

TO MAKE THE CUSHION

1 To work the embroidery mount the white Aida fabric
onto your frame ensuring the fabric grain is parallel to the
sides of the frame. Find and mark with tacking (basting)
stitches the centre hole of the fabric.

2 Work the embroidery using three strands of thread at
all times. Work the centre section first and then the rich
outer border around this.

Ensure all your cross stitches are constructed in the
same way to give a neat and even effect. Also check every
now and then to make sure your stitching is accurate, as
it is quite easy to jump a square without noticing, putting
the whole design out of alignment. The tacked (basted)
guidelines and the simple border pattern around the centre
section will help you with this.

Once you have completed the stitchery remove the
fabric from the frame.

3 To make the cushion, accurately count twenty-four
sets of threads or squares out from the outer edge of the
border pattern to establish the seam line. Mark with a pin

on each side. Count outwards across another six sets of
threads and accurately cut along this line on each side to
trim away the excess fabric from the cushion front.

4 Place one of the white cotton backing squares under
the wrong side of the embroidered fabric. Join the layers
by accurately machine straight stitching in white sewing
thread along the marked seam line.

5 Place the remaining white cotton backing square
under the wrong side of the printed cotton square (to add
support to the fabric). Then with right sides together
place the embroidered fabric over the printed fabric so
that the backing layers are outermost. Pin, tack (baste)
and machine straight stitch accurately along the seam line,
starting at one corner and finishing off half-way along the
fourth side to leave an opening.

6 Trim the layers of fabric across the corners of the
seam allowance and carefully turn the cushion to the right
side. If necessary press the cover gently on the wrong
side to remove any creases that may have occurred.

7 Place the cushion pad inside the cover. Fold in the
edges of the opening and slip stitch to close, leaving a
small gap at the corner. Do not finish off the thread at
this stage.

8 Tuck one end of the decorative cord into the tiny
opening at this corner, taking care that the cord does not
unravel. With matching thread (double thickness for extra
strength) slip stitch the cord around the cushion. When
you arrive back at the starting point cut off the excess
cord allowing a small amount to be pushed neatly into
the seam gap. With a little patience you will find you can
make the cord appear to be continuous. Close the seam
line gap with your white sewing thread and finish off
neatly.

NOTE: Some cords unravel quickly when cut. To prevent
this happening bind the cut ends either with thread or
temporarily with adhesive tape.

HELLEBORE & IVY CUSHION

DMC STRANDED COTTON

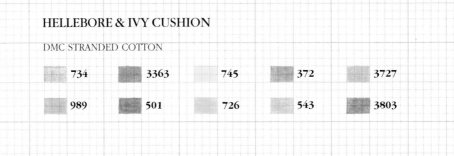

734	3363	745	372	3727
989	501	726	543	3803

HELLEBORUS HANGING SACHET

THIS ELEGANTLY SHAPED SACHET will not only brighten your bedroom or guest room but its sweet aroma will pervade the air delightfully. Worked quickly and easily within a hoop the design takes only a short time to complete.

MATERIALS

White Aida fabric (Zweigart E3706), 14-count, 10in (25cm) square

Printed cotton fabric for back of sachet, 8in (20cm) square

White cotton backing fabric, two pieces each 8in (20cm) square

DMC stranded cotton (floss): 1 skein each Green 501, 989, 3363; Maroon 3803; Pink 543, 3727; Mustard 734; Light Brown 372; Yellow 726, 745

White sewing thread

Gathered white cotton lace edging, ⅜in (2cm) wide, 20in (50cm) long

Small amount of Terylene or polyester filling

Small amount of pot-pourri

Smoky-pink satin ribbon, ⅛in (3mm) wide, 36in (90cm) long

Pink sewing thread to match ribbon

Wooden embroidery hoop, 8in (20cm) diameter

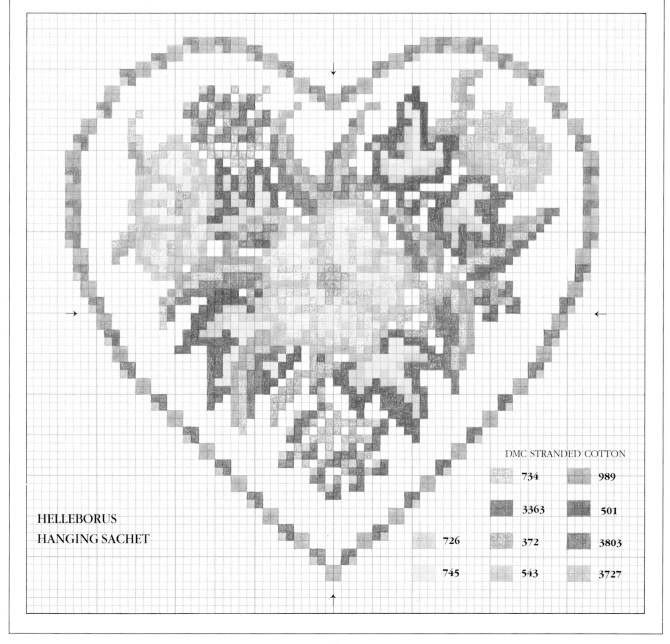

HELLEBORUS
HANGING SACHET

DMC STRANDED COTTON

734		989	
3363		501	
726	372		3803
745	543		3727

TO MAKE THE SACHET

1 Place the white Aida fabric centrally within the hoop ensuring the grain of the fabric is straight. Find and mark with tacking (basting) stitches the centre hole of the fabric.

2 Work the embroidery using three strands of thread at all times, working from the centre of your design outwards, completing the design with the border pattern. When completed, remove the fabric from the hoop and carefully press it on the wrong side with a steam iron.

3 Make a traced paper pattern of the heart shape below, accurately marking the cutting line and the seam line. Trim away the excess paper leaving just the heart shape. Pin this centrally over the embroidered motif and cut carefully around the shape. Remove the paper pattern, carefully trim around it following the seam line markings.

4 Place one of your white cotton backing squares under the wrong side of the Aida heart. Pin the trimmed paper pattern centrally over this, aligning it carefully with the stitched shape and pinning through all the layers.

5 With white sewing thread machine straight stitch the two fabric layers together using the cut edge of the paper pattern as your guide. Remove the pattern.

6 Pin the gathered lace edging along the seam line, carefully arranging the fullness of the gathers to follow the shape of the heart, allowing extra gathers at the point of the heart shape. Tack (baste) the lace in position.

7 With right sides together place the printed fabric over the sachet front and then add the remaining white cotton backing square. Pin to hold all the layers together. Carefully turn over the layers to see the heart-shaped seam line. Stitch along this once more, leaving an opening of about 2¼in (6cm) along one side. Take care not to catch the fullness of the lace in the stitching.

8 Trim away the excess fabric leaving a narrow seam line, carefully clip the seam allowance at the points of the heart. Turn the sachet to the right side and gently ease it into shape. Press gently on the wrong side if necessary.

9 Place the filling inside the sachet adding some potpourri at the same time. Turn in the raw edges of the opening and close with neat and tiny slip stitches.

10 Arrange the narrow ribbon so that there are six loops (all approximately the same size) and two end tails. Then using matching thread (double thickness for extra strength) carefully and securely stitch the looped ribbon to the centre top of the heart sachet to complete.

seam line
cutting line

To use this as your paper pattern, enlarge the heart shape by 150 per cent using a photocopying machine

WINTER GARDEN BATH LINEN

*T*HE SOFT BUTTERY COLOUR *of the bath linen (see page 103) adds a feeling of warmth to this beautiful border design. Even the face-cloth has a simple band of cross stitches to co-ordinate with the towel. The border design is a repeat pattern, easily adapted to any length. It would also look stunning made into tiebacks to hold a voile or muslin curtain, or perhaps hung as a decorative bell pull.*

MATERIALS

White Aida fabric (Zweigart E3706), 14-count, 6 x 24in
  (15 x 60cm)
DMC stranded cotton (floss): 2 skeins Green 989; 1 skein
  each Green 501, 3363; Maroon 3803; Pink 543, 3727;
  Mustard 734; Light Brown 372; Yellow 726, 745
Pale yellow hand towel, 20in (50cm) wide
Pale yellow face-cloth to match
White sewing thread
Yellow sewing thread to match towel
Small rotating frame

TO WORK THE BORDERS

I used a small rotating frame to embroider the borders as I prefer to work on a taut or semi-taut surface. The fabric remains crumple-free and it is easy to keep the stitching neat and even. However, it is possible to work these borders freely in the hand or in a small hoop, but do take care to keep the excess fabric rolled up and clean.

1 Mount the ends of the long strip of Aida fabric onto the rotating sides of the frame and roll the excess fabric onto one of the rollers.

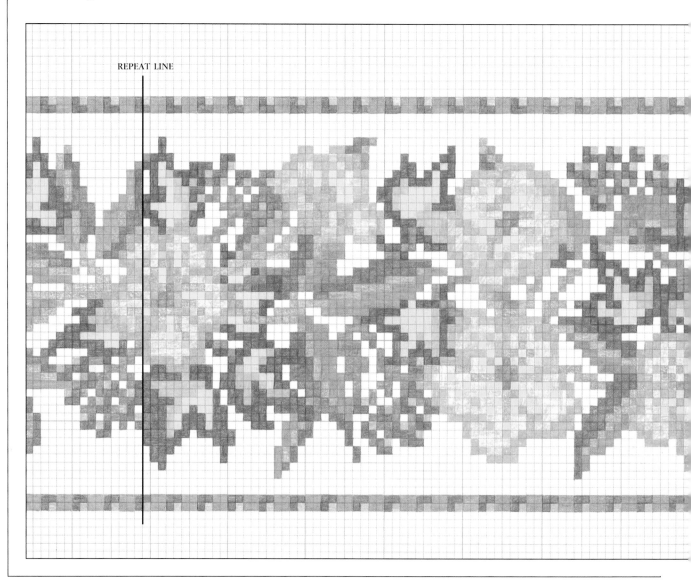

REPEAT LINE

2 Using three strands of embroidery thread at all times, start stitching the towel border approximately ¾in (2cm) away from the end of the Aida strip. Then count eight sets of threads in from the side of the strip to give you the position of the green and maroon border pattern. This off-centre positioning of the towel border on the fabric will enable you to work the face-cloth pattern parallel to the towel border.

Continue to work the repeat pattern along the fabric until your border is slightly longer than the width of the hand towel.

3 Before removing the fabric from the frame work a length of the simple border pattern to measure a little more than the width of the face-cloth, positioning it centrally between the cut edge of the fabric and the towel border edge. (You need to allow eight sets of threads between the stitching of both borders.)

Once your stitching is complete remove the fabric from the frame. If necessary press on the wrong side with a steam iron.

4 Carefully trim away the excess fabric leaving four sets of Aida threads along each side of both the towel and face-cloth borders. Trim the excess fabric from the ends of the strips, leaving a small turning allowance at the ends.

5 Place the wide border strip across one end of the hand towel so that it covers the woven band. Pin and tack (baste) in position, tucking in the raw ends between the border and the towel.

6 With white sewing thread on top of your sewing machine and yellow thread in your spool (bobbin) work a line of wide satin stitch along both edges of the border, covering them with the width of the stitching. This will neatly and securely attach the embroidered strip to the towel.

7 Neatly slip stitch the tucked-in ends of the bands to the towel sides.

Attach narrow border to the face-cloth in the same way.

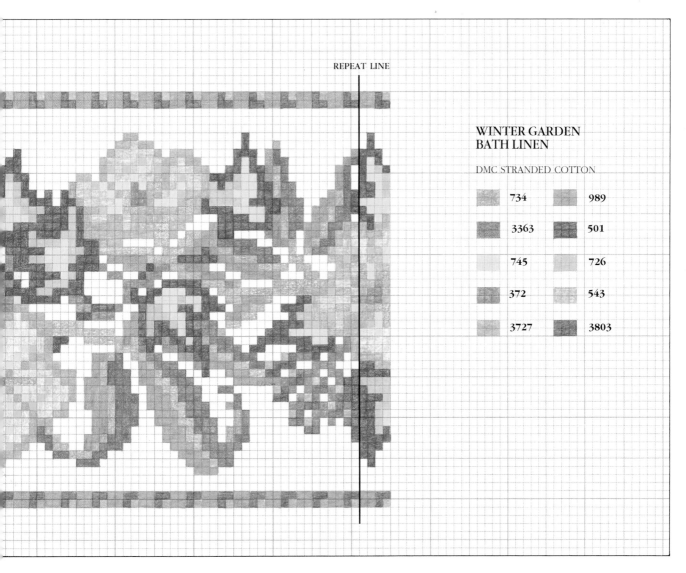

REPEAT LINE

WINTER GARDEN BATH LINEN

DMC STRANDED COTTON

	734		989
	3363		501
	745		726
	372		543
	3727		3803

WINTER CIRCLETS

PERIWINKLES AND ACONITES PROVIDE the inspiration for these simple but elegant circlets, which can be used as place mats (opposite) or jar covers. Larger or smaller designs can be made by altering the fabric gauge. If you do alter the design size remember to re-calculate the amounts of materials required.

MATERIALS

For both circlets

White Aida fabric (Zweigart E3706), 14-count, two pieces each 10in (25cm) square

DMC stranded cotton (floss): *for periwinkle circlet* – 1 skein each Green 501, 989; Maroon 3803; Pink 543, 3727; Mustard 734; *for aconite circlet* – 1 skein each Green 501, 989; Yellow 726, 745; Maroon 3803; Mustard 734

White cotton lace edging, 2¼yd (2m) by ⅝in (1.5cm) wide

White sewing thread

Satin ribbons for jar covers

Wooden embroidery hoop, 8in (20cm) diameter

TO MAKE THE CIRCLETS

The circlets are both worked in the same way.

1 Place the fabric centrally in the hoop ensuring the grain is straight. Find and mark with tacking (basting) stitches the centre hole of the fabric.

2 Work the embroidery using three strands of thread at all times. Carefully count outwards from the centre hole to commence stitching the design. When the stitching is complete remove the fabric from the hoop and press it gently on the wrong side with a steam iron.

3 Make a paper pattern of a circle 6in (15cm) in diameter. Place this centrally over the wrong side of the embroidered circlet then lightly draw around the pattern with a light coloured crayon and trim away the excess fabric.

4 Cut the lace edging into two halves. Gather one half to fit around the raw edge of the trimmed circlet. Carefully and securely attach the lace to the edge of the fabric using a neat line of wide machine satin stitch. (You may wish to practise this step on a scrap of fabric before working on the edge of the circlet.) Hand stitch the raw ends of the gathered lace together so that the join is inconspicuous.

5 If using the circlets as jar covers use a length of toning satin ribbon to secure around the top of the jar or pot, tying into a bow.

For trinket boxes and matching cards see page 110

PERIWINKLE CIRCLET

DMC STRANDED COTTON

	734		989		501
	543		3727		3803

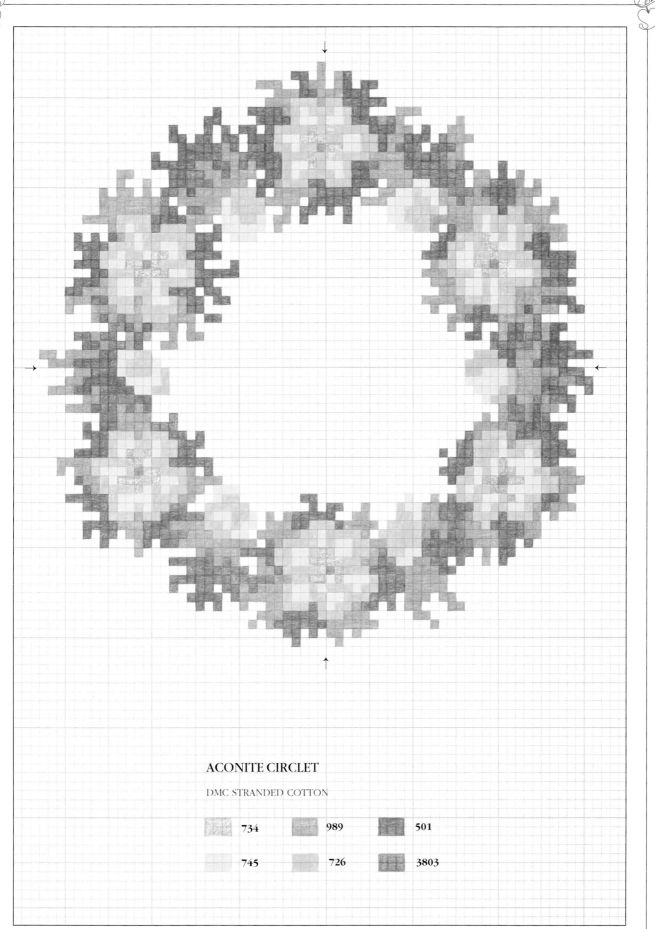

ACONITE CIRCLET

DMC STRANDED COTTON

	734		989		501
	745		726		3803

TRINKET BOXES &
GIFT CARDS

*T*HE CHARMING LITTLE DESIGN *motifs echo the colours used in the larger projects of the winter collection and are stylised clusters of flowers and foliage arranged into circlets and a tiny all-over geometric pattern. You can adapt them by choosing a different set of coloured threads, for example by replacing the shades of pink and maroon with perhaps blue and lilac or red, green and gold for Christmas boxes.*

TRINKET BOXES

The attraction of these beautiful trinket boxes is that they make such wonderful gifts but only take a short time to prepare and put together. You could make the gift even more special by working a matching gift card, which can then be mounted in a miniature frame (see below).

MATERIALS
For both trinket boxes
White Aida fabric (Zweigart E3706), 14-count, 8in (20cm) square
DMC stranded cotton (floss): small amounts Green 501, 989; Maroon 3803; Pink 3727; Yellow 726, 745
Wooden embroidery hoop, 7in (18cm) diameter
Two porcelain trinket boxes, DMC Creative World, Ivory N850 1¼in (3cm) diameter and N851 2⅝in (6.5cm) diameter

TO MAKE THE TRINKET BOXES
You can work the two designs for the trinket boxes within one hoop at the same time as there is plenty of space, but do plan the positioning carefully, making sure there is approximately 1½in (4cm) between the outermost stitches of the designs to allow for cutting and mounting.

Use three strands of thread making sure all cross stitches are constructed in the same way.

1 Place the fabric within the hoop ensuring the grain is straight. When each motif is complete remove the fabric from the hoop and if necessary press it on the wrong side to remove any creases.

2 Following the manufacturer's instructions, trim the excess fabric from around each motif and mount them within the lids of the trinket boxes.
NOTE: I chose to mount the fabric in the lids without the use of the protective acetate circles as I wanted the stitchery to stand out. If you choose to do this remember that the fabric and threads will become dusty and a little soiled over time and that laundering is not possible.

GIFT CARDS AND TAGS

These beautiful little cards will certainly bring joy to whoever receives them. Like the trinket boxes they are so quick and simple to make and mount and use the same fabric and threads. I used DMC Chelsea Studio Cards, Christmas Green N2394 and Cream N2399 to mount the motifs.

Try to experiment with the motifs. For example the all-over pattern motif can be worked to fit a different shape (see small square motif card on page 106). Once again you can achieve original variations simply by choosing a different colour scheme or working on a larger or smaller gauge fabric.

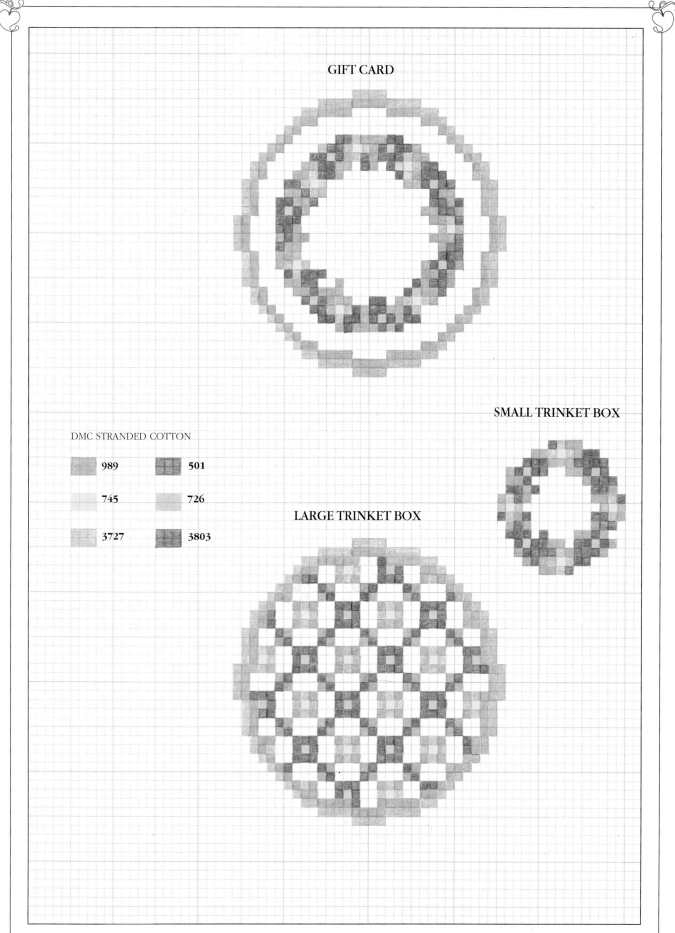

GIFT CARD

SMALL TRINKET BOX

DMC STRANDED COTTON

989		501	
745		726	
3727		3803	

LARGE TRINKET BOX

CHAPTER 8

The Christmas Garden

THE CROSS STITCH COUNTRY Garden would not be complete unless it included a Christmas Garden with its wealth of tradition just waiting to be used. By the month of December most of our gardens will be predominantly dormant with only small jewel-like pockets of colour showing. So what could be better than to sit in the warmth of your home and stitch these delightful projects, so that when Christmas does arrive not only can you decorate your home with sprays of berry-laden holly, ivy and mistletoe, but also with some of these cheering designs.

The master design in this chapter is the Christmas Garden Picture, from which most of the other designs are derived. It is composed of four sparkling, festive motifs, each edged with a crisp border to form a delightful picture. As you can see I have chosen the very strong shades of red and green that are associated with Christmas, adding hints of gold, yellow, brown and blue to make my design vibrant with simple images of topiary bushes, wreaths, baskets of foliage and, of course, Christmas trees. The family of projects created from this main design include gift tags, tree decorations, festive bath and table linen. All of the designs can be adapted easily for all sorts of ideas. The majority of the projects shown are quickly completed making them ideal to embroider at the onset of such a busy time of year.

CHRISTMAS GARDEN PICTURE

I CAN REMEMBER VERY clearly that special moment each December when the appearance of a rather dusty and very old cardboard box, tied up with great care and labelled 'decorations' heralded the arrival of the festive season. This box was filled with all sorts of treasures, some quite new and still glittering, others tarnished with age, all well-loved. I hope that this strikingly simple Christmas picture will evoke the same sense of anticipation for you and your family when it is hung each year.

MATERIALS

Cream 264 Hardanger fabric (Zweigart E1008), 22-count, 16in (40cm) square

DMC stranded cotton (floss): 2 skeins each Green 701; Blue 3807; 1 skein each Green 907; Tan 3828; Red 606; very small amount Yellow 742

DMC divisible metallic thread, D282 Light Gold, 1 spool

Firm mounting cardboard, approximately 11in (28cm) square, or to fit frame

Strong buttonhole thread, any colour

Wooden frame with 10½in (26.5cm) square aperture (without glass). I chose a limed pine-finish frame with a subtly carved decorative pattern

Wooden rectangular frame, 15in (38cm) square (or other suitable frame)

TO MAKE THE PICTURE

1 Start by stretching the Hardanger fabric over the frame, ensuring the grain is straight and parallel to the sides of the frame.

2 Find and temporarily mark with tacking (basting) stitches, the centre of the fabric so that your stitches intersect each other over a centre hole.

3 Use three strands of embroidery cotton (floss) and a double length of gold thread and make sure all the stitches are worked to face the same way. Each cross stitch is worked over two horizontal and two vertical sets of threads so that although it is a 22-count fabric you will only produce eleven cross stitches to every inch (2.5cm), giving a fairly large-scale stitch which is quick to grow.

Starting in the centre of the design and working outwards and around the edges, work the Green (701) border pattern. This, once worked, gives you the basic framework within which the four motifs are placed. Accuracy at this early stage is absolutely vital, so check and double check that you have counted and worked the correct number of Green cross stitches.

After completing this outer border gradually build up the rest of the design. You may choose to work one motif square at a time or all four simultaneously.

4 Once the design is complete remove the tacking (basting) stitches and take the fabric off the frame. If necessary press the edges of the fabric on the wrong side to flatten them ready for mounting.

5 Use strong buttonhole thread to lace the fabric centrally over the square of mounting cardboard (see Basic Stitches and Techniques, page 15). Now place the stretched embroidery within the purchased wooden frame.

NOTE: You may prefer to have your embroidery professionally stretched and framed but remember this will be much more expensive.

The motifs from the Christmas Garden Picture have been worked on small squares of perforated paper to make delightful tags or tree decorations (see page 117)

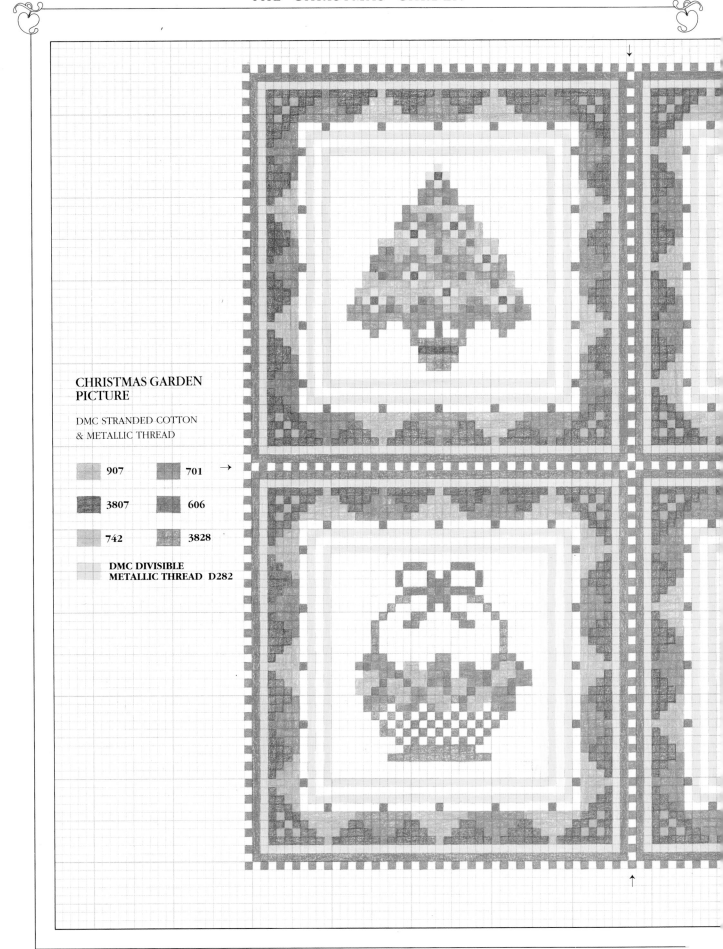

CHRISTMAS GARDEN PICTURE

DMC STRANDED COTTON
& METALLIC THREAD

907	701	→
3807	606	
742	3828	

DMC DIVISIBLE METALLIC THREAD D282

GIFT TAGS & TREE DECORATIONS

THESE BEAUTIFUL TAGS ARE quickly and easily worked on small pieces of perforated paper which is becoming much easier to buy in good craft shops and is wonderful to use to make small items such as these. Each tag has as its motif one of the four Christmas images used in the Christmas Garden Picture. A border of three colours, chosen to compliment the motif, complete each design.

MATERIALS

White perforated paper (stitching paper), four pieces each 3½in (9cm) square

DMC stranded cotton (floss): 1 skein each Green 701, 907; Blue 3807; Tan 3828; Red 606

DMC divisible metallic thread D282, Light Gold, a small amount

Tiny gold beads, approximately 100

Sharp paper scissors to trim the perforated paper

TO MAKE THE TAGS OR DECORATIONS

Perforated paper is easy to use holding it carefully in the hand but do remember not to pull the thread quickly or tightly through the holes as the paper will tear if handled roughly, especially when using the gold thread (see Materials and Equipment, page 11).

1 Use three strands of cotton (floss) and a double thickness of gold thread and work all your cross stitches to face the same way. Work the four Christmas motifs from the chart shown here, centrally within each of the small squares of paper. Add a scattering of tiny gold beads over the green foliage areas of the design.

2 Work a three-colour border around each motif. Stitch the inner coloured band in the same position as the inner gold border on the chart. Then work the next colour of your choice and finish off with another band, this time in gold.

3 Trim away the excess paper, cutting along the next row of holes around the embroidery.

4 To complete each tag or decoration cut two lengths of gold thread each approximately 8in (20cm) long. Thread them together through the top centre gold cross stitch of the outer border. Tie the ends of the gold thread together to complete.

If you want your gift tag to convey a message then add a self-adhesive label or glue a piece of paper very carefully to the wrong side of the tag.

FESTIVE PILLOW & MATCHING GUEST TOWELS

THESE GORGEOUS TOWELS AND charming scented pillow make ideal gifts but would also look stunning in a guest room to welcome friends and relatives at Christmas time. Look closely and you will see their designs have been taken from the Christmas Garden Picture.

MATERIALS

To make the pillow and two guest towels

Gold/Fleck Aida fabric (Zweigart E3287), 14-count, ready-cut pack 12in (30cm) square

DMC stranded cotton (floss): 1 skein each Green 701, 907; Tan 3828; Red 606

DMC coton perlé No 5 thread, 1 skein Red 606

White cotton backing fabric, two pieces each 6in (15cm) square

Christmas design cotton fabric, one piece suitable for back of pillow, 6in (15cm) square

Cream gathered cotton lace edging, ¾in (2cm) wide, 24in (60cm) long

Two small, green guest towels, 11in (28cm) wide

Sewing thread, red, cream and green to match towels

Small amount of Terylene or polyester filling

Small amount of pot-pourri

NOTE: I have used an Aida fabric that has woven within it a sparkling gold Lurex thread, making it ideal for these festive projects. The fabric is conveniently available in ready-cut pieces of different sizes. The Lurex thread in the Aida fabric gives an extra firmness to the fabric so I found it suitable to hand hold without using a frame. However, do take care not to crumple the fabric and handle it as little as possible. You may of course use a suitable frame if you wish.

TO MAKE THE PILLOW

1 If necessary press the Aida fabric gently on the wrong side to remove any fold marks. Measure and cut two strips each 2in (5cm) wide by the width of the fabric and reserve these for the guest towel borders. Trim the remaining piece of fabric to become an 8in (20cm) square. (Reserve the excess piece for some other project idea.) Carefully find the centre stitch and temporarily mark with tacking (basting) stitches.

2 Work the embroidery (see chart on page 120) using three strands of embroidery thread at all times. You will find it beneficial to work outwards from the central motif, completing your design with the outer border – this helps to avoid counting errors.

3 If you have used a hoop remove the fabric from it and carefully press it on the wrong side using a steam iron. Count ten sets of threads from the edge of the outermost tan line of stitches and cut along this line on each side to trim away the excess fabric.

4 Place one of the white backing squares under the Aida fabric and machine straight stitch around your design with cream sewing thread along the seam line, which is four sets of threads away from the outer tan line of cross stitches. Pin the gathered lace edging along this seam line.

5 Place the remaining backing square under the Christmas design fabric and pin together. With right sides facing, pin and tack (baste) these layers to the prepared Aida square, ensuring that the fullness of the gathered lace edging is not caught in the seam line at the corners. Machine straight stitch along the seam line remembering to leave an opening of approximately 2¼ in (6cm) along one side.

6 Trim the seam allowance across the corners and turn the pillow to the right side and gently ease into shape. Press gently on the wrong side with a steam iron if necessary. Place your filling and pot-pourri inside the pillow, then turn in the raw edges of the opening and close by hand with tiny slip stitches. Join raw ends of lace to neaten.

7 Make a twisted cord using four lengths of the coton perlé thread. Carefully unravel the skein of thread and cut off four lengths each measuring 72in (183cm). Tie the threads together at each end and use to make the cord (see Basic Stitches and Techniques page 14).

8 Stitch the cord around the pillow using red sewing thread, starting and finishing at the bottom right corner. As you start to stitch the cord leave a loose hanging tail (with a knotted end) at least 2½in (6.5cm) long. Similarly leave the same amount hanging when you arrive back at this point. Neaten the cord ends with mock tassels by teasing out the cut thread ends. Arrange the hanging cords to look like a small bow and stitch into position.

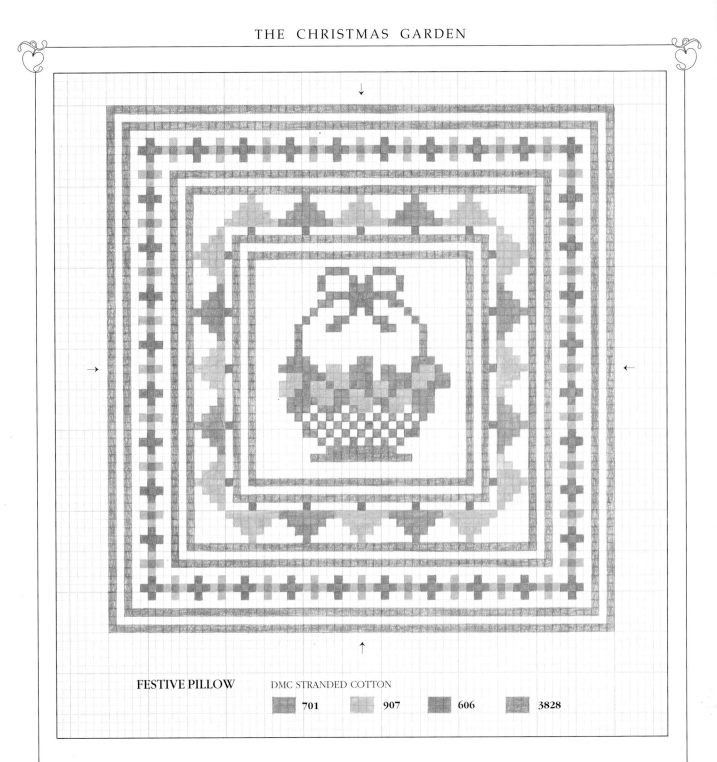

FESTIVE PILLOW   DMC STRANDED COTTON

701   907   606   3828

TO WORK THE TOWEL BORDERS

1 These simple but striking border strips are worked freely held in the hand and are quick to complete. Work each border pattern centrally along your 2in (5cm) wide Lurex Aida strips, repeating the simple Christmas tree motif or the tiny flower over and over again to cover the length of each fabric strip (see chart above). When complete press gently on the wrong side with a steam iron to remove any creases.

2 Carefully trim away the excess fabric along each side of the border pattern leaving a minimum of two sets of threads on each edge as a turning allowance. (You may wish to leave more to make a wider border.)

3 Pin and tack (baste) a border to each towel, tucking in the turning allowance at the ends. Then, with cream sewing thread on the top of your sewing machine and green on the bobbin (spool), machine satin stitch along the raw edges of the border, covering them completely with the width of the stitches and attaching the border strip to the towel securely.

4 Finally, slip stitch the turned allowances to the towel sides to complete your guest towels.

TOPIARY GREETINGS CARDS & WALL PICTURES

DMC STRANDED COTTON

701   907   606   3828

TOPIARY GREETINGS CARDS & WALL PICTURES

I ALWAYS MARVEL AT the sight of beautifully crafted bushes that have been lovingly trimmed into shape. To me they always convey a cheerfulness and a sense of well-being so it seemed very appropriate to take this idea as part of my design theme for the Christmas Garden. As you can see there are four shapes of bush each growing proudly from identical pots, and decorated with tiny gold beads to add that special touch of luxury that Christmas permits.

MATERIALS
For each design
Cream 264 Hardanger fabric (Zweigart E1008), 22-count,
   8in (20cm) square
DMC stranded cotton (floss): small amounts of Green 701,
   907; Red 606; Tan 3828
Tiny gold beads, approximately 15 per card/picture
Sewing thread, gold coloured
Wooden embroidery hoop, 6in (15cm) diameter, optional

Additional materials to make a greetings card
Greetings card (DMC Chelsea Studio Card, N2392),
   Christmas red or green
Strong clear adhesive suitable for fabric and card

Additional materials to make a wall picture
Firm mounting cardboard approximately 4⅜ x 6in
   (11 x 15cm) or to fit inside chosen frame
Strong buttonhole thread, any colour
Wooden frame with a 5 x 7in (12.5 x 17.5cm) aperture
Dark green cardboard mount to fit frame with 3½ x 5in
   (9 x 12.5cm) aperture
NOTE: The limed-pine frame and window mount I chose
are both a standard size available ready-made from many
craft, home interior and photographic shops.

TO WORK THE TOPIARY MOTIF

1 Place the Hardanger fabric centrally in the hoop ensuring the grain is straight. Find the centre stitch of your working area and mark with tacking (basting) stitches.

2 Use three strands of thread at all times and remember to construct all the cross stitches to face the same way. Following the charts on page 121, commence stitching the topiary bush of your choice, completing the design with the red and green border pattern.

3 Using gold coloured sewing thread and a fine needle, securely stitch the tiny gold beads randomly over the foliage area of the bush.

4 When your stitching is complete remove the fabric from the hoop and if necessary press gently on the wrong side with a steam iron.

TO ASSEMBLE THE CARD

1 Open out the card and use it to help you measure and then trim away the excess fabric from around the embroidered design, so that your fabric is ⅝in (1.5cm) bigger all round than the window shape.

2 Glue the fabric in place behind the window mount. Then glue the right-hand section of the card to the back of the embroidery in the window section and write your message on the inside of the left-hand section.

TO MOUNT THE PICTURE

1 Place the embroidered fabric over the mounting card so that the embroidery is centred. Trim away any excess fabric leaving at least 1in (2.5cm) turning allowance on each side. Use strong buttonhole thread to lace the fabric over the cardboard (see Basic Stitches and Techniques page 15).

2 Place the stretched embroidery in your chosen frame with the cardboard mount.

The clarity and simplicity of these designs makes them very effective on the cream Hardanger fabric seen here and also on the green fabric of the table setting seen on page 125. If you wish though you can vary the designs, perhaps making only very subtle changes, such as reversing the border pattern as in the red card or by making bolder changes such as working the ribbon in blue or the plant pot in gold thread

CHRISTMAS TOPIARY TABLE LINEN

CHRISTMAS IS THE TIME of year when we all try to make our dinner table look as attractive as possible, so why not create a really stunning table setting with these beautiful table mats, napkins and holders which are decorated with elegant topiary bushes. I have chosen bold plaid woven mats and napkins to set off the rich colours of the embroidery but a plain colour can be equally as effective.

With a little experimentation and adaptation you could effectively use one of the beautiful linen bands that are available. You will need one which gives an odd number of stitches across its width as the topiary bushes are predominantly symmetrical on either side of a centre line of stitches. If you purchase 36in (90cm) of your chosen linen band you will have enough for one place mat and napkin holder and have some left over on which to experiment. You may find you have to adapt the border design, making it narrower, or if you use one of the bands with a coloured edge you may choose to omit the cross stitch border altogether.

The quantities given below are enough to decorate one place mat and matching napkin holder. (NOTE: The napkin matches the place mat but is left undecorated.) If you wish to make more then calculate carefully how much extra fabric and other materials you will need.

MATERIALS
Christmas Green 685 Hardanger fabric (Zweigart E1008), 22-count, 8 x 20in (20 x 50cm)
DMC stranded cotton (floss): 1 skein each Green 701, 907; Red 606; Tan 3828
Red plaid place mat and matching napkin (mat to measure 13½in (34cm) deep)
Green sewing thread to match Hardanger fabric
One small clear plastic press-stud
Small rotating frame

TO MAKE A PLACE MAT AND NAPKIN HOLDER

1 Mount the short ends of your Hardanger fabric on the rotating sides of the frame and roll the excess fabric around one of these sides.

2 Divide the fabric in half widthwise by tacking (basting) stitches. This will enable you to work the decorative strip for the place mat and the strip for the napkin holder side by side, leaving enough fabric to line the napkin holder.

3 Use three strands of embroidery thread at all times. Position both designs centrally within the thin area of fabric you have allotted for them and no less than 1in (2.5cm) away from the cut fabric end attached to the rotating frame.

4 The exact size of the place mat may vary from the one used here, so lengthen or shorten your strip as necessary by working more or less of the border pattern above and below the topiary bushes. For a 13½in (34cm) deep mat work 1½in (4cm) of the border pattern and then commence the three-tier topiary bush (see chart on page 126). Continue working the design along the fabric strip leaving a gap of five squares (stitches) before repeating the bush motif once more. On reaching the lower end of the design work a further 1½in (4cm) of the border pattern to complete – this will allow for a small turning.

5 Now work the napkin holder motif in the other half of the fabric, starting on a level with the beginning of the place mat stitchery (see chart on page 126). Choose which bush shape you wish to work. If you are going to make several holders then why not work all the different bushes?

6 Once you have completed the stitchery remove the fabric from the frame and press on the wrong side using a steam iron.

7 Carefully trim along the outer edge of the place mat border strip, leaving four sets of threads beyond the red border stitches. Allowing for a small turning at each end of the strip, trim across the top and bottom. Place the strip approximately 1in (2.5cm) away from the right edge of the place mat. Pin, tack (baste) into position, tucking in the cut ends between the place mat and the Hardanger fabric.

8 With matching green thread, machine satin stitch along the sides of the border covering them completely with the width of the satin stitches, thus attaching the strip to the place mat. Finally, slip stitch the turned allowance neatly to the top and bottom edges of the mat.

9 To make the napkin holder trim away the excess fabric around the embroidered strip leaving eight sets of threads on each side around the red line of stitches. Use this as a template to cut out a matching shape from the remaining fabric, remembering to cut along the grain of the fabric. With right sides together place the two pieces of fabric together and pin to hold.

10 On all sides, count out from the edge of the red border across four sets of threads – this will be the seam line. Machine straight stitch along this line with matching thread, leaving the top short end open. Carefully clip across the seam allowance at the corners and turn the fabric to the right side and gently ease into shape. If necessary press the napkin holder on the wrong side with a steam iron. Tuck in the seam allowance at the open end and close with small, neat slip stitches.

11 Finally, stitch one half of the clear plastic press-stud on the wrong side of the napkin holder centrally behind the base of the cross stitch flowerpot, making sure your stitches do not show through to the right side. Align the other half of the press-stud on the right side at the other end of the holder so that when the studs are pressed together the napkin holder forms a ring to hold the napkin.

CHRISTMAS TOPIARY
TABLE LINEN

DMC STRANDED COTTON

▨	701	▨	606
▨	907	▨	3828

ACKNOWLEDGEMENTS

I would like to thank everyone who has helped in the making of this book. There are too many to name individually but I would like to mention the following in particular.

Di Lewis for her wonderful photography and Margaret Foster for her delightful book design.

I must express my immense gratitude to everyone at DMC Creative World Ltd, especially to Cara Ackerman for all her generous support, advice and the never-ending supplies of fabrics, threads, cards and trinket boxes, which I have gained so much pleasure from using throughout this book.

Thanks also to Woodhouse, for their beautiful wooden items, and to Sylvia for her friendly and helpful advice, to Jane Judd my agent, to Vivienne Wells and to Cheryl Brown at David & Charles for all their encouragement and understanding.

A special thanks goes to Alison Edwards, my hardworking and ever-helpful friend, who enthusiastically embroidered several of my designs.

Finally, thank you to my very tolerant family and my mother for all their help and patient understanding. It has been greatly appreciated as without them my task would have been far less pleasurable.

SUPPLIERS

DMC Creative World Ltd, Pullman Road, Wigston, Leicestershire LE18 2DY
DMC threads, wools, Zweigart fabrics, cards, trinket boxes, information.

John Lewis, Oxford Street, London W1A 1EX
Cotton fabrics, upholstery fabrics, towelling, bed linen, embroidery threads, ribbons and lace, trimmings, sewing threads and general haberdashery.

Farnworths, Unit 37, The Glades Shopping Precinct, Bromley, Kent BR1 1DD
Also at Lakeside, Thurrock, Brighton, Cardiff.
Picture frames and card mounts.

Woodhouse, Rock Channel, Rye, East Sussex TN31 7HJ
Mail order – woodwork footstools, pincushions.

INDEX